Velocity Warm-Ups

92 Improvisational Patterns for Jazz Vibraphone and Marimba

By CHARLES DOWD

AF173930

EL 3172

Photos by Harry B. Houchins

ABOUT THE AUTHOR

Charles Dowd is a performing vibist whose training includes doctoral work at The Juilliard School in New York City, Masters degree from Stanford University and the Bachelors degree from San Jose State University. A frequent studio percussionist on the west coast, Mr. Dowd has appeared at jazz festivals throughout the USA, leads his own jazz quartet, and appears regularly as a timpanist and percussionist under many name conductors with the Cabrillo Music Festival, the Eugene Symphony Orchestra in Oregon and others. His recently released LP CHARLES DOWD: SOLO VIBES/SOLO DRUMS has won acclaim nationwide. Mr. Dowd is an artist clinician with Ludwig-Musser Industries and the Avedis Zildjian Company, and is currently Associate Professor of Music at the University of Oregon in Eugene in Percussion and Jazz Studies.

CONTENTS

FOREWORD

"In this era of the total musician it is becoming increasingly necessary for today's musician to be able to cover the whole musical spectrum from Bach to Boulez, Jelly Roll Morton to Frank Zappa to The Police.

The mallet playing percussionist is no exception. One is often called upon in all the myriad musical situations to be able to competently execute jazz passages on mallet instruments. Charles Dowd's book offers a practical and logical method for "putting your chops together". The serious student and the professional has much to gain by reading and practicing the material in this book. One could not help but benefit by including this in his/her daily creative practice regimen."

.....John Prince

John Prince is a renowned jazz composer and musician who writes regularly for the Tonite Show. He has also written for NBC and ABC special programming, Disneyland, Magic Mountain and special material for actor Bill Cosby, musicians Flora Purim, Doc Severinsen, Jerome Richardson, Clare Fischer, Ed Shaughnessy, Raoul de Souza and many others. In addition, he has written for many colleges and had his works featured in national and international jazz festivals where he has also appeared as a clinician, soloist and adjudicator. Over the past ten years John Prince has developed a course of study in the commercial music field at Cal State University Long Beach offering a unique and creative Bachelor of Music Degree in Commercial Music with a concentration in Performance.

FROM THE AUTHOR

This collection of velocity warm-ups is from one performer to another. These are warm-ups for the mallet player that are derived from a tonal vocabulary of today's jazz: pentatonics, modal jazz, arpeggios and scale structures relating to "playing changes" and other elements. Here in a single collection I have attempted to provide warm-up studies in a current improvisational vocabulary, each with two purposes: 1) to provide scales/chords/modes that are **practical** and in use by leading players and composers, and 2) to provide stickings that allow a mallet player to grow and master state-of-the-art technique.

In my own attempt as a performer to improvise solos freely, keep up my "chops" and play written music accurately and musically, I find this collection of warm-ups helpful. If these velocity studies can increase another player's speed, flexibility and endurance in a regular practice routine, sharing them has been worthwhile.

Best Wishes in Your Practice

Charles Dowd

To **David Friedman and David Samuels.**

Music preparation by Anthony Kaye.

INTRODUCTION

TO THE STUDENT

Select a specific exercise, read it, then memorize it. Keep a steady tempo starting slowly, working up to a very fast speed. Try to keep relaxed at all times. Try to maintain an even volume, keeping the right and left sounding the same. Strive to phrase each exercise, and avoid playing the exercise mechanically. Always try to play your scales and modes musically, even though the purpose is technique. If you memorize all this material, and are in the habit of phrasing and playing musically, your improvised solos will be relaxed and free. Be sure to listen to a lot of music, focusing on the jazz solos of the well recorded mallet players as well as the jazz greats of all instruments. Remember that technique is only one part of musicianship. For best results use these daily. Select material to solve a particular weakness, rather than using the book in numerical order.

TO THE TEACHER

The student should master the alternating stickings first, since much mallet music lays well using alternating sticking. Advanced players, however, find re-working all the scales and modes using "mixed stickings" adds a whole new dimension and freedom to their playing. Therefore, there are no "correct" stickings. Usually the best choice of sticking is the one that lays best, is most comfortable, uses the least motion and is most logical. One should master the entire book with alternating stickings, then master the book using the mixed stickings. Professional mallet players argue whether one can play faster and more relaxed using alternating sticks versus mixed sticking. Ideally, the student should feel comfortable with either choice. These warm-ups are but a few of the many exercises one can use, and represent a starting point from which the student should move to other books on jazz improvisation and four mallet technique.

TO THE PROFESSIONAL MALLET PLAYER

One can perform the entire book of exercises in about forty five minutes of continuous, relaxed velocity playing. Invent additional exercises. These work well on xylophone as well as vibraphone and marimba. If you are in the habit of sticking a particular passage or scale a certain way, there are stickings herein that may seem very awkward at first. Keeping an open mind to new trends keeps a performer fresh. Use these warm-ups before going on stage to perform. For the classical mallet player, many of the patterns jazz and studio percussionists use will also work well for the classical xylophone and marimba repertoire. For the jazz player, whether one thinks about it or not, most of the scale and modal structures are quite common in the music. Learn new and different structures to keep the ideas fresh. These velocity warm-ups may help keep the boredom out of keeping the hands and mind in shape!

How To Use "Velocity Warm-Ups for Jazz Vibraphone"

Each exercise is written in a certain key, **only to let the performer know how it goes, to enable memorization.** Start each exercise from the lowest note on the instrument, then play it chromatically up through the highest range of the instrument (or vice versa). While the first seven pages can be played with just two mallets, many players hold all four mallets while playing single line melody. Therefore, **The entire book is meant to be a "four mallet book"**, allowing the performer to use mallet no. 1 (right hand) and mallet no. 3 (left hand) playing single line exercises while keeping mallet no. 2 (right hand) and mallet no. 4 (left hand) as motionless as possible. (Further explanation of technical materials can be found on page fifty eight). Often, well developed vibists will **not** lay two mallets down when playing single line improvisations, but will hold all four mallets even though only the two "melody mallets" are needed (#s 1 and 3).

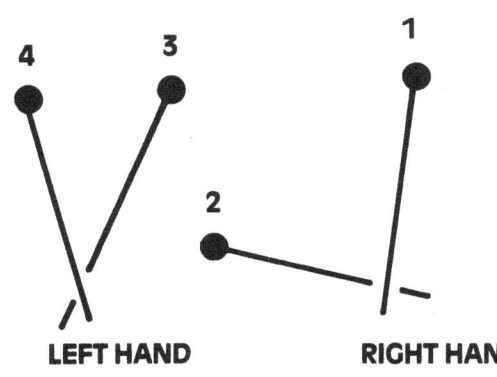

LEFT HAND   **RIGHT HAND**

When playing single line melody, mallet no. 1 will "arc stroke" (mallet no. 2 will "pivot"), mallet no. 3 will "arc stroke" (mallet no. 4 will "pivot"). Play the book **without any pedal** or with only "half pedal" to develop clarity in the line. Further description and photos of this can be found in the book **"Four Mallet Studies"** by Gary Burton.

MAJOR SCALES

Play these next five pages continuously as one exercise, once they are memorized. Move onto each new scale without repeating the starting note of the preceding scale. Use alternating stickings when playing the complete exercise. After mastering pages 8 through 12 with alternating stickings, re-learn the exercise using mixed stickings.

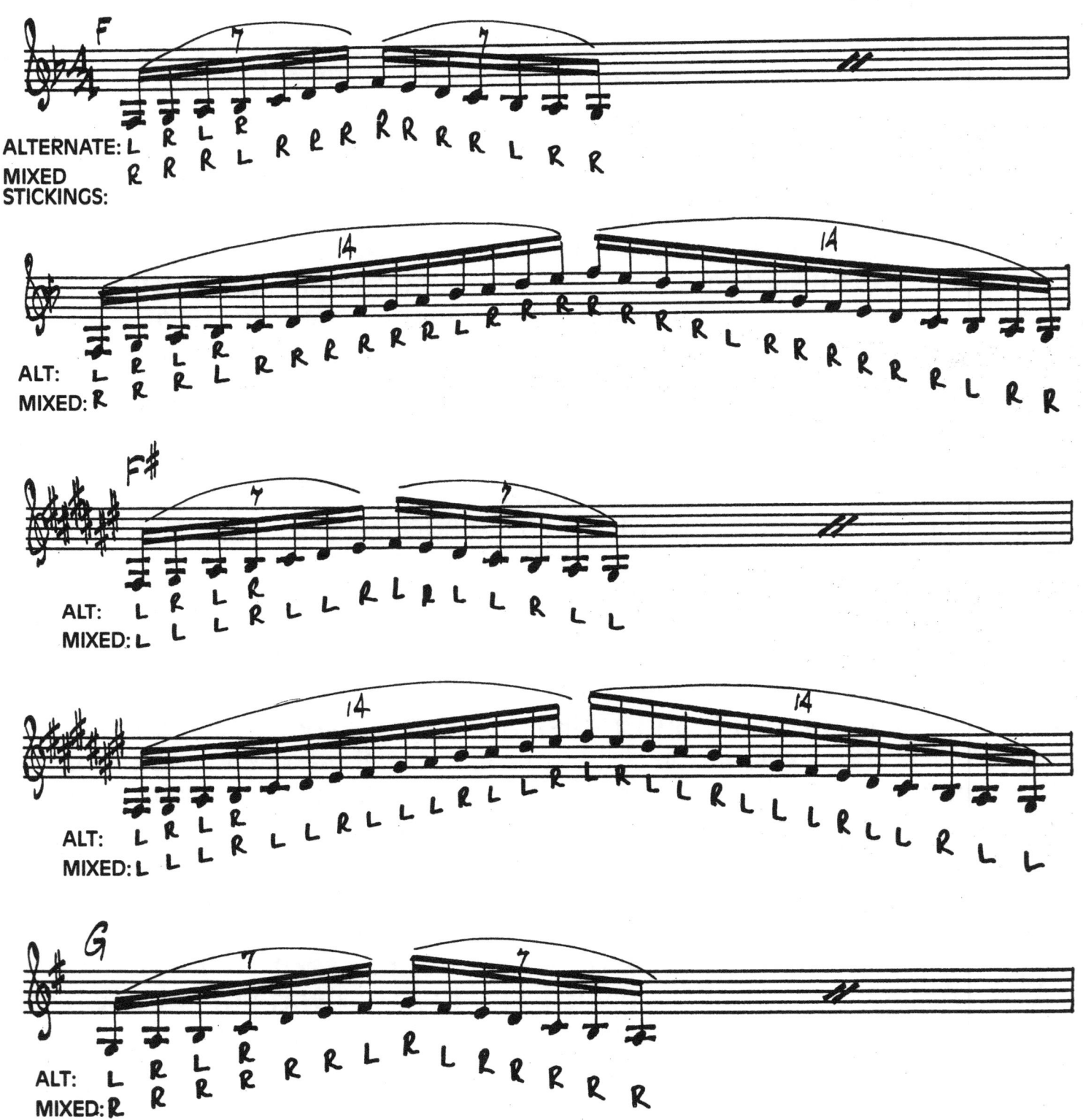

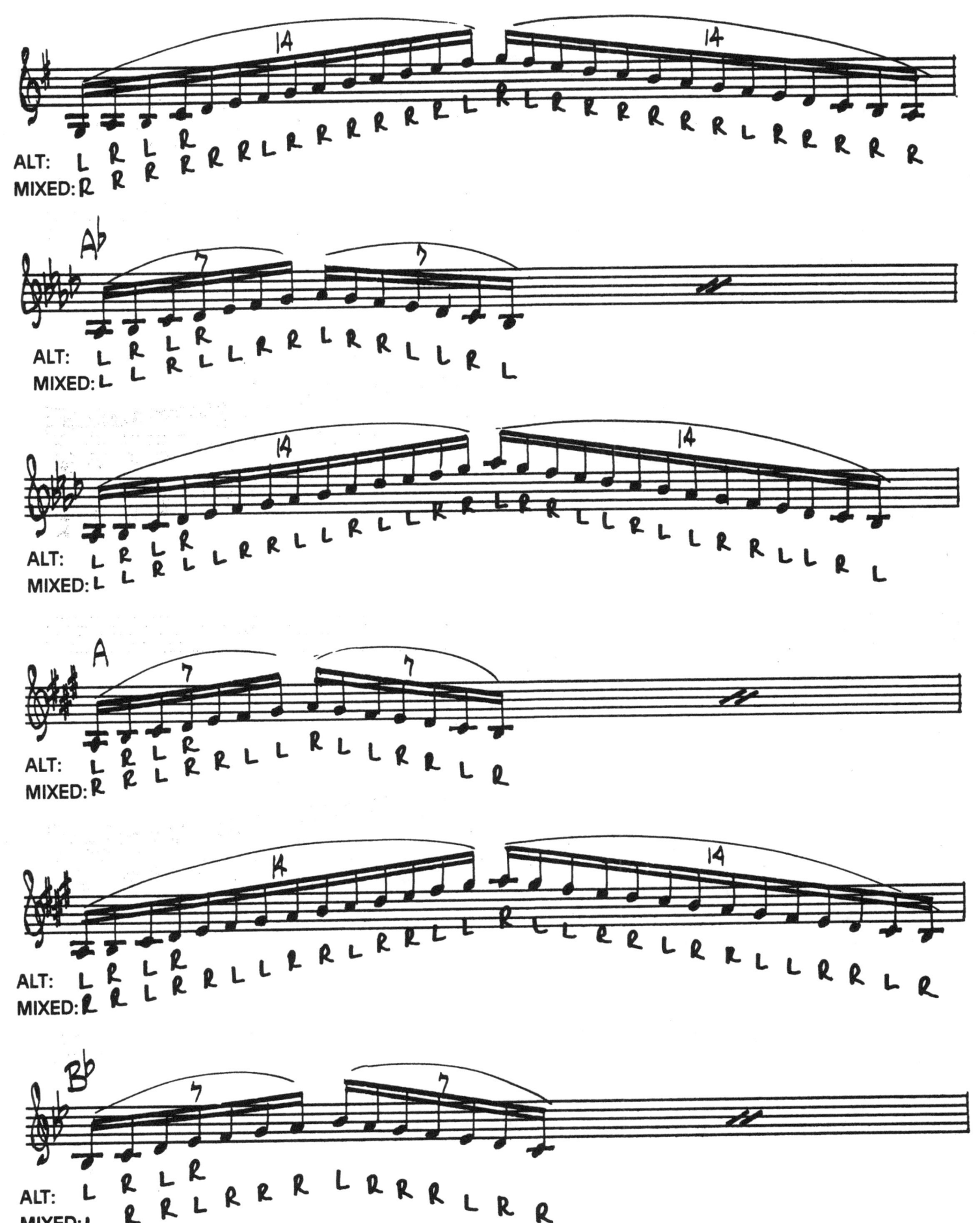

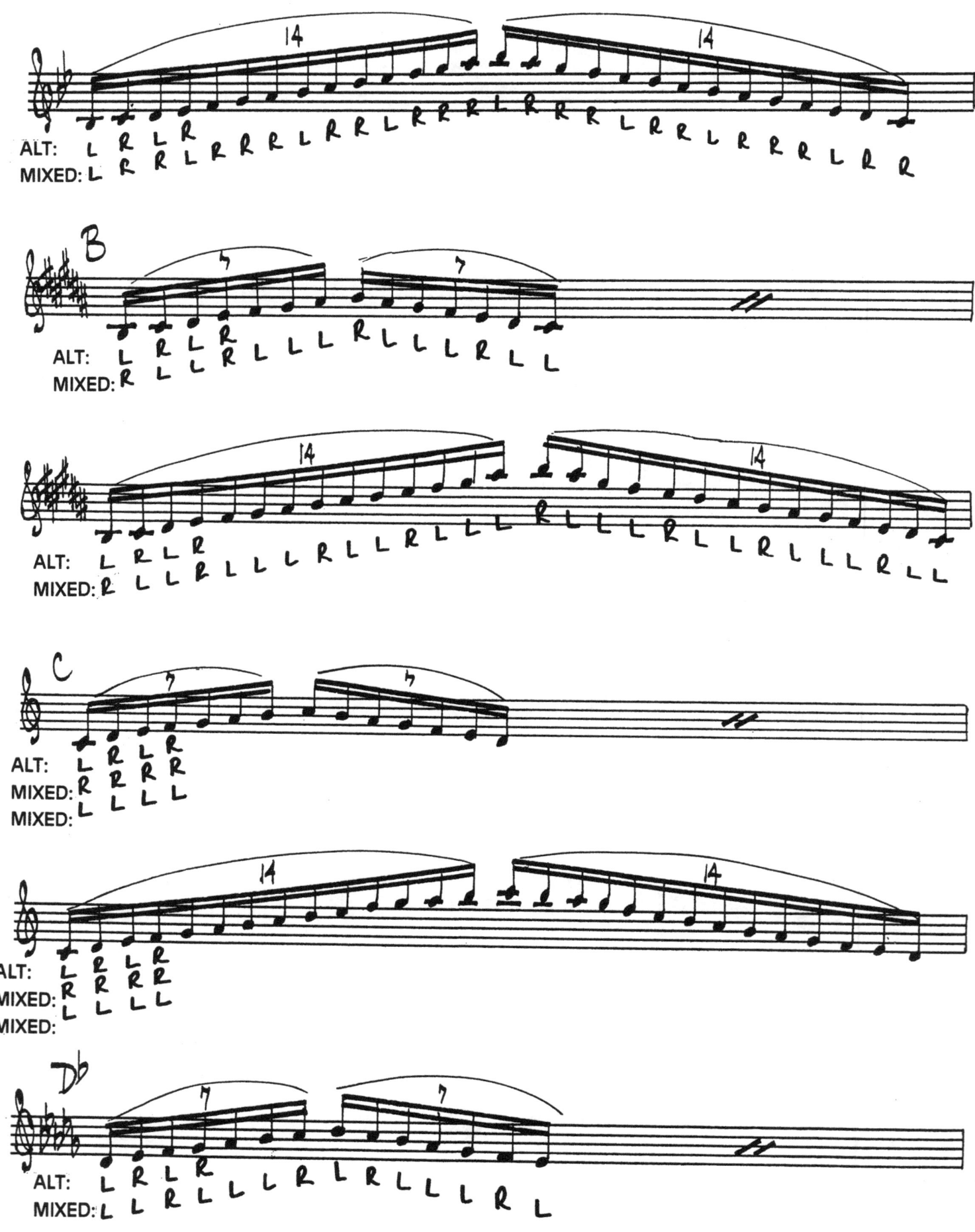

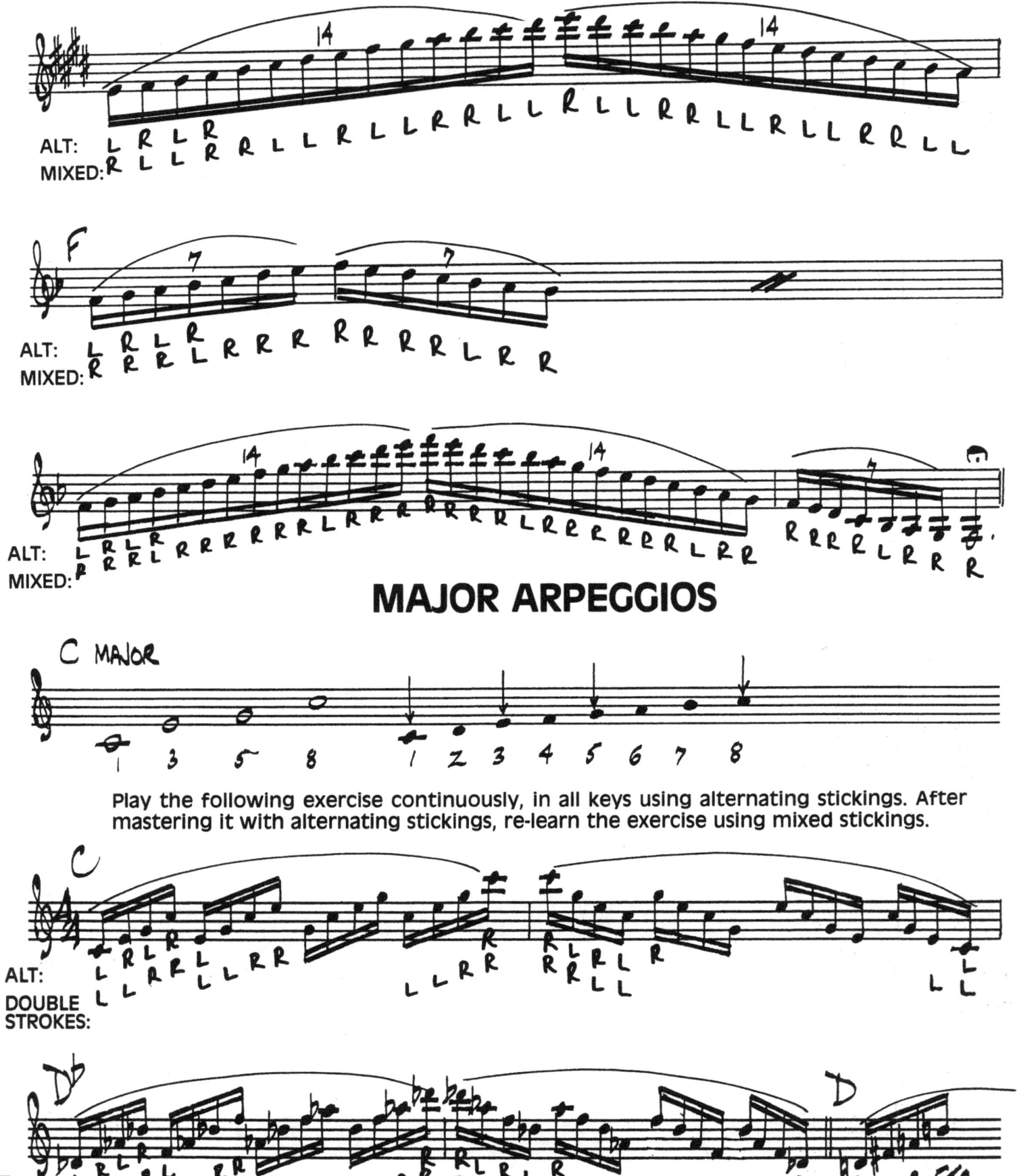

MAJOR ARPEGGIOS

Play the following exercise continuously, in all keys using alternating stickings. After mastering it with alternating stickings, re-learn the exercise using mixed stickings.

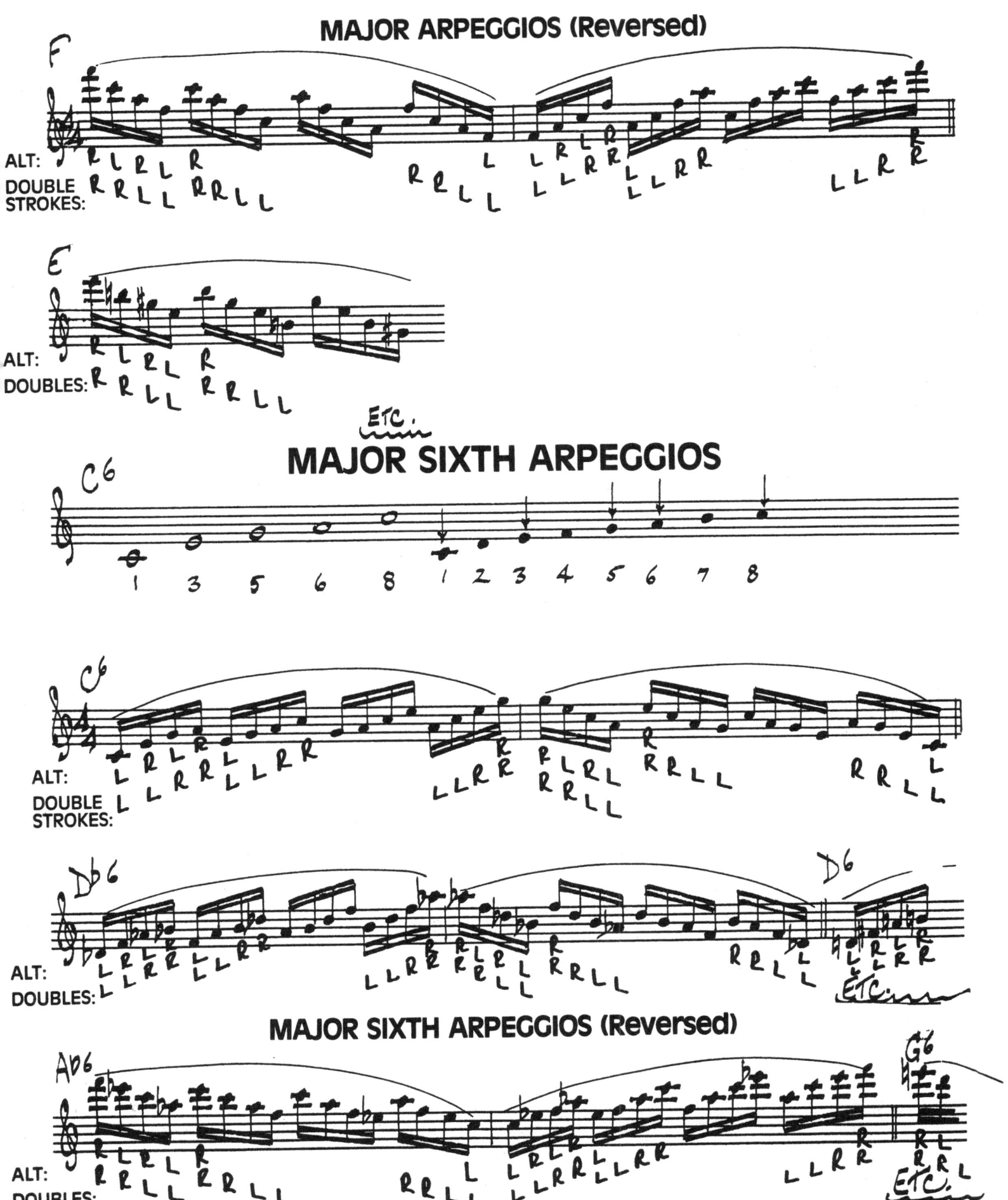

MAJOR SEVENTH ARPEGGIOS

MAJOR SEVENTH ARPEGGIOS (Reversed)

DOMINANT SEVENTH ARPEGGIOS

DOMINANT SEVENTH ARPEGGIOS (Reversed)

DOMINANT THIRTEENTH ARPEGGIOS

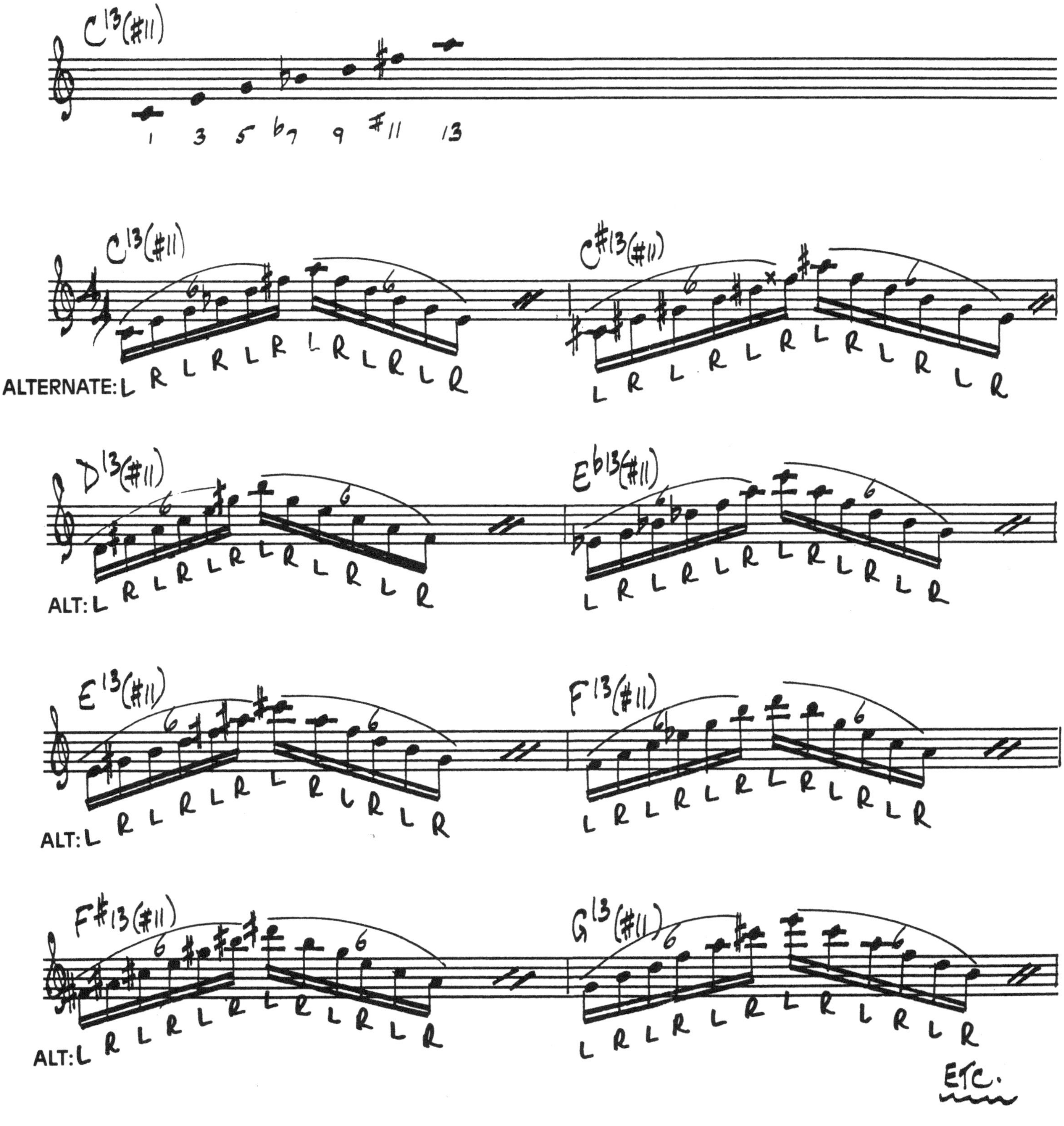

MIXOLYDIAN MODES

Play these next five pages continuously as one exercise, once they are memorized. Move on to each new scale without repeating the starting note of the preceding scale. Use alternating stickings when playing the complete exercise. After mastering pages 16 through 20 with alternating stickings, re-learn the exercise using mixed stickings.

ALTERNATE: L R L R L R L R L R R L R R

MIXED
STICKINGS: R R R L L R R L R L R L R R

ALT: L R L R L R R L R R L R R L R R L R R L R L R R L R L R R
      R R R L L   R R

F#7

ALT: L R L R L R L L R L R L L R L L
      L L L R L R   L

ALT: L R L R L L L R L L L R L R L R L L L R L L L R L L R L L
      L L L R L R   R L L

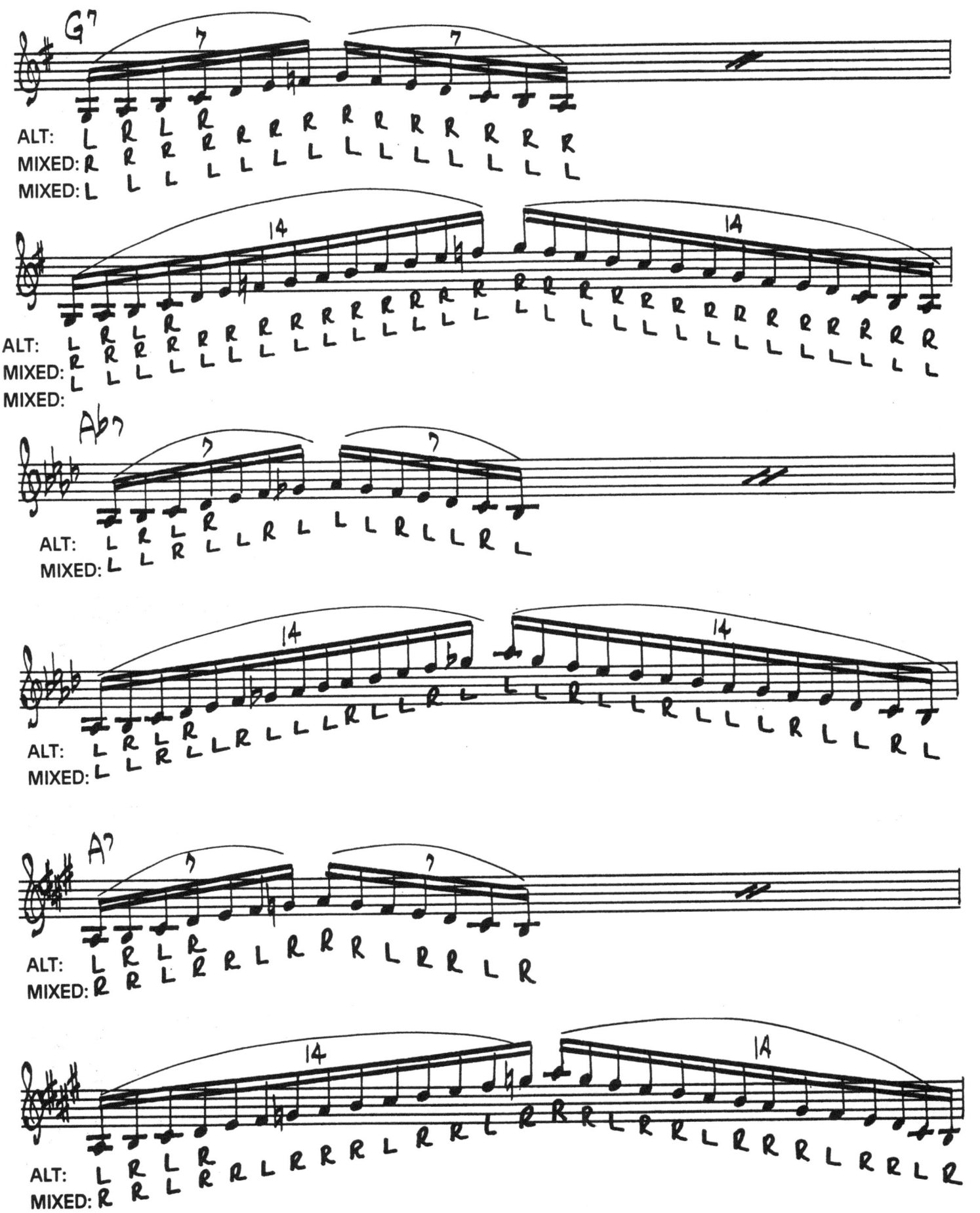

18

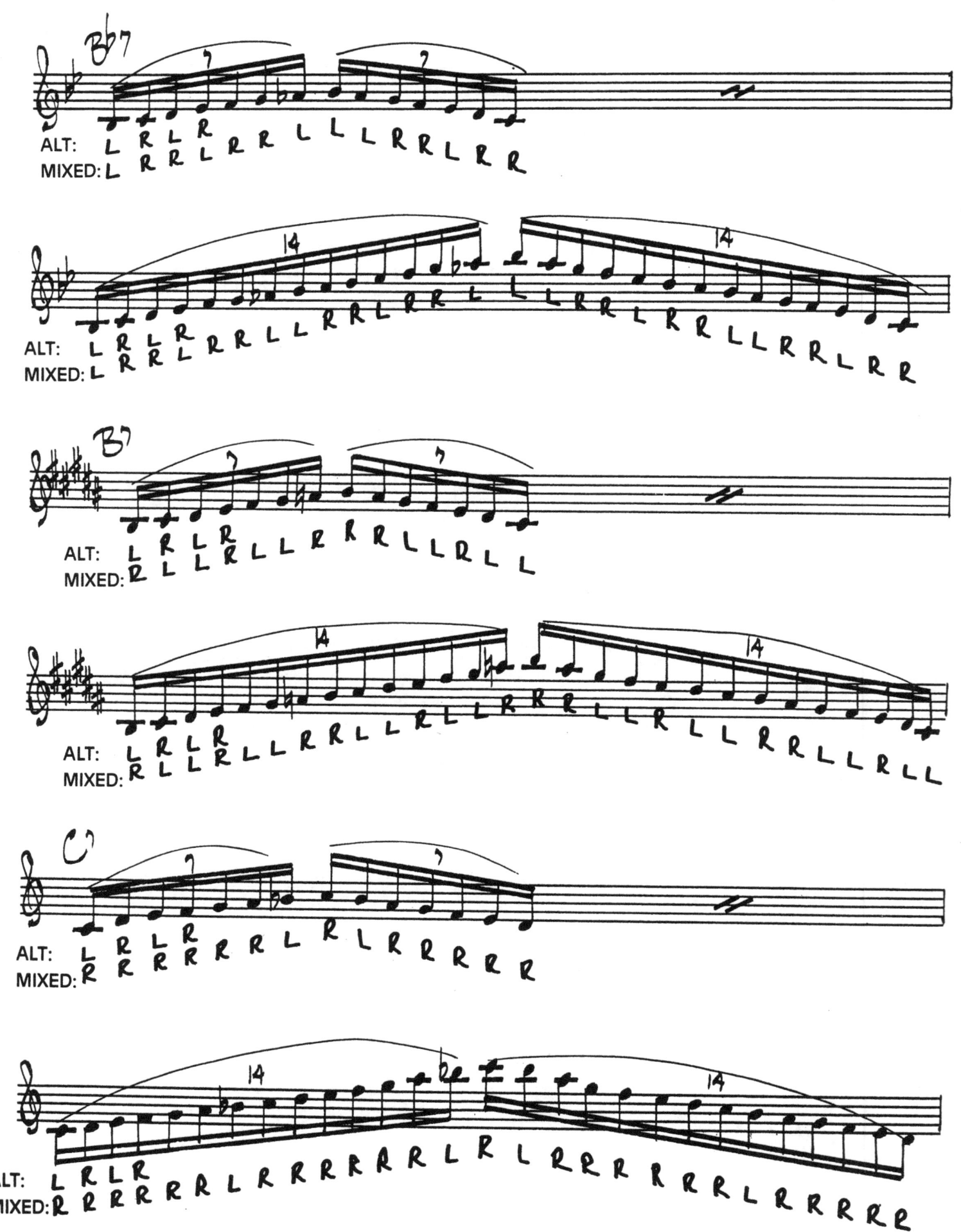

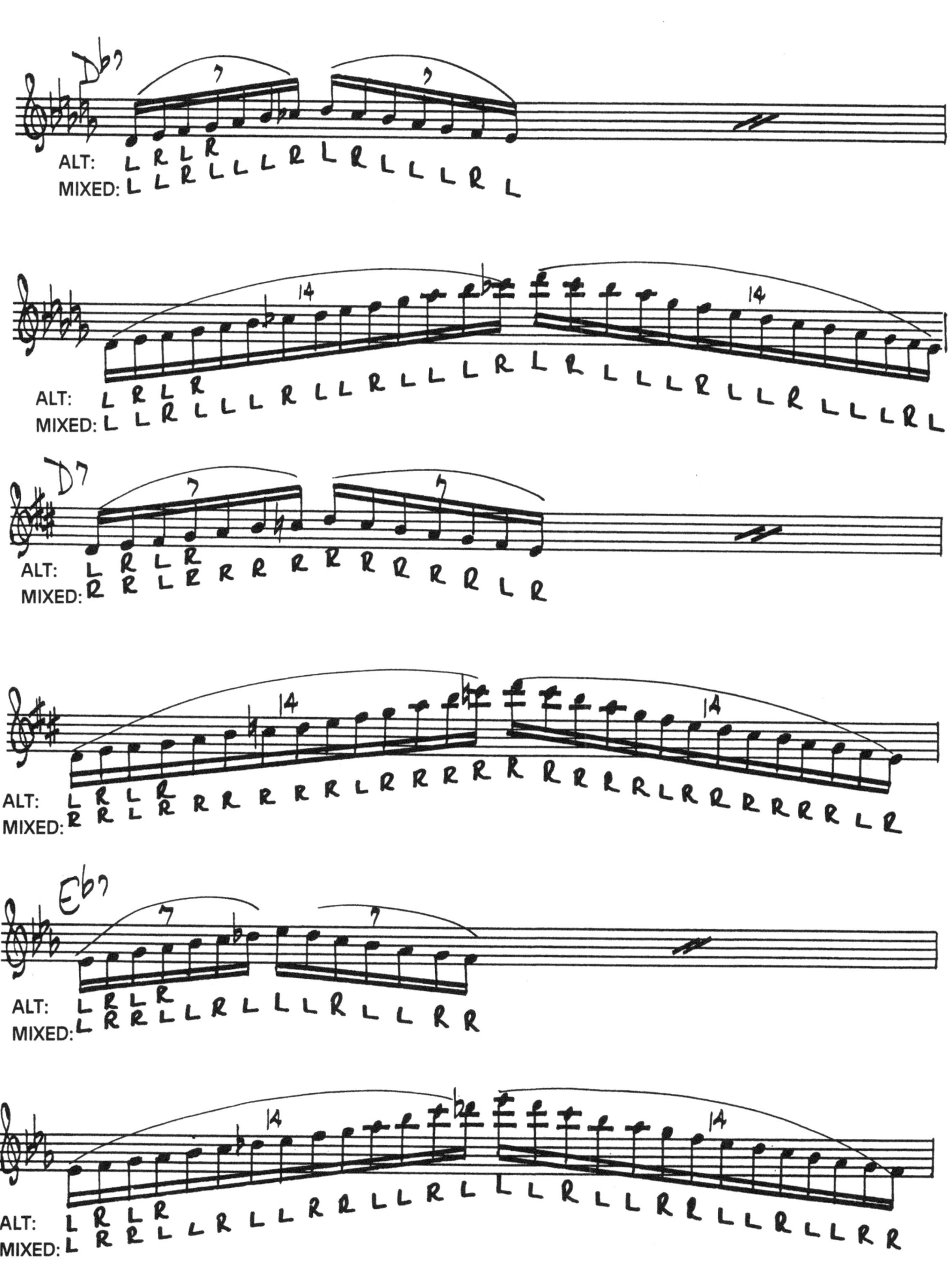

BLUES SCALES (One Octave)

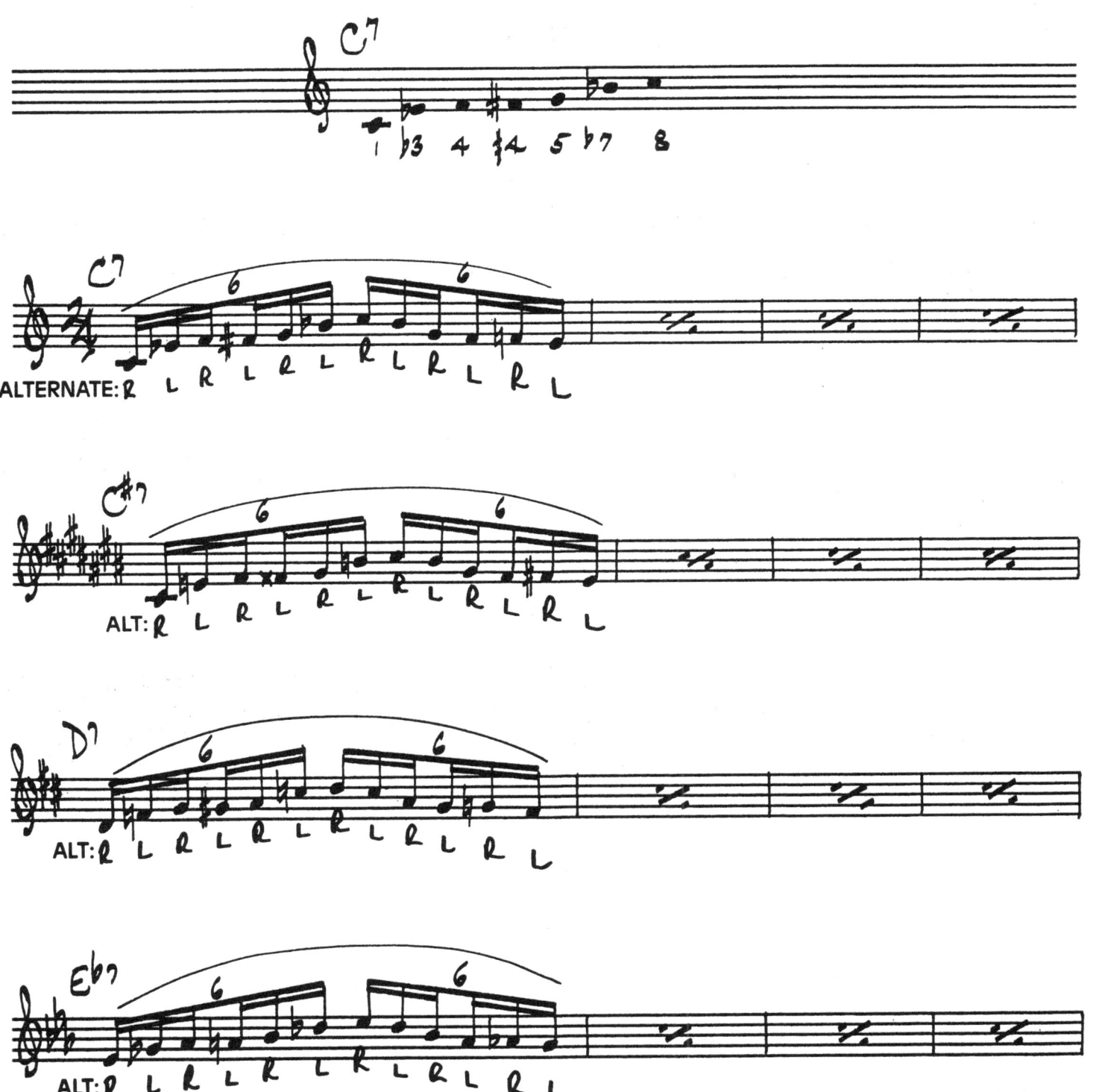

PLAY IN ALL KEYS

BLUES SCALES (Two Octaves)

ETC. PLAY IN ALL KEYS

HARMONIC MINOR SCALES

Play these next five pages continuously as one exercise, once they are memorized. Move on to each new scale without repeating the starting note of the preceding scale. Use alternating stickings when playing the complete exercise. After mastering pages 23 through 27 with alternating stickings, re-learn the exercise using mixed stickings.

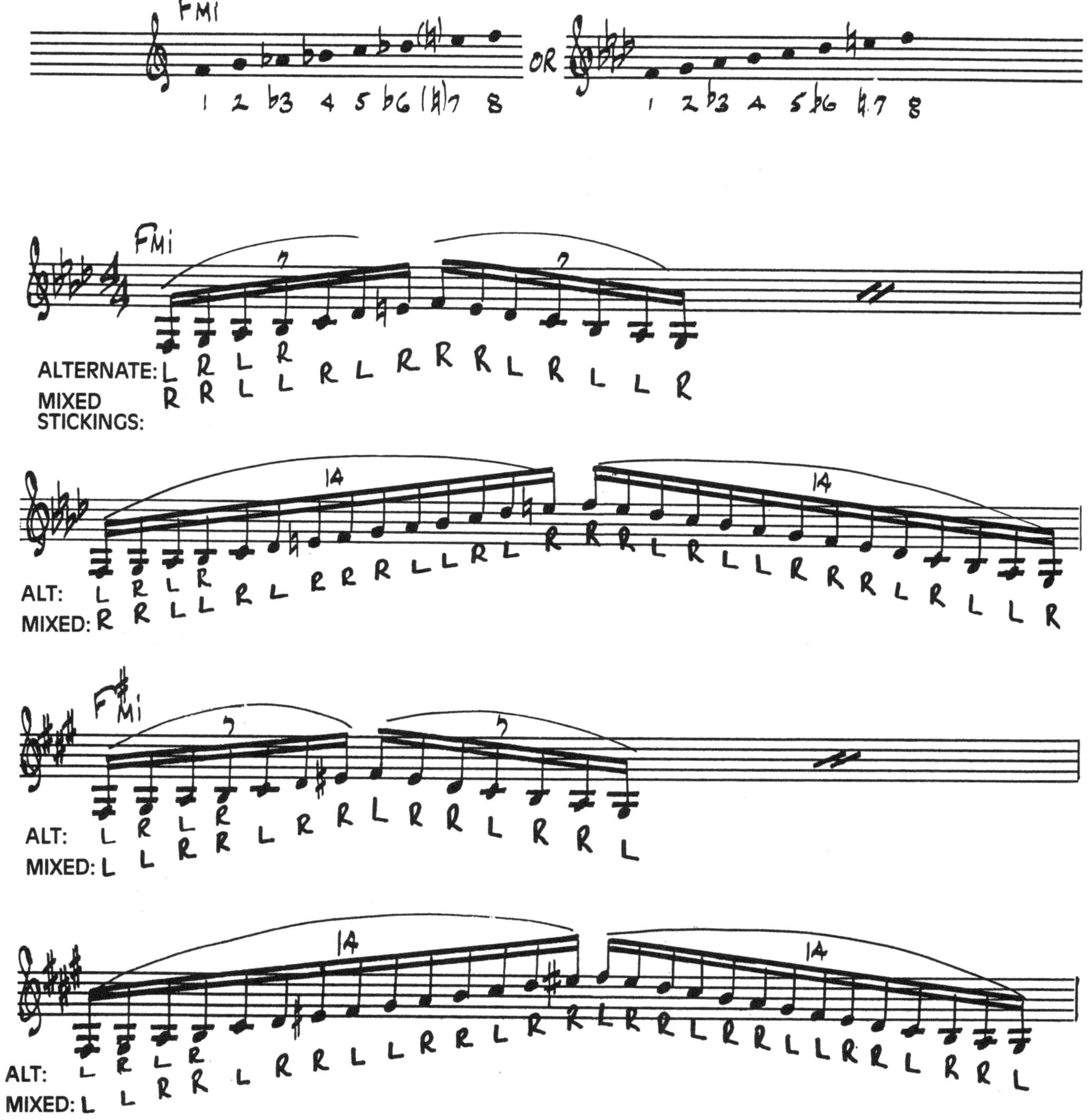

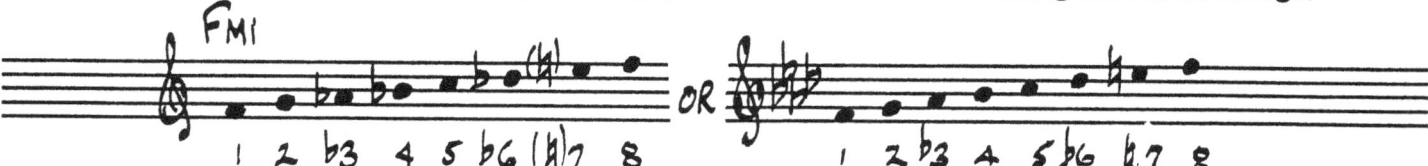

24

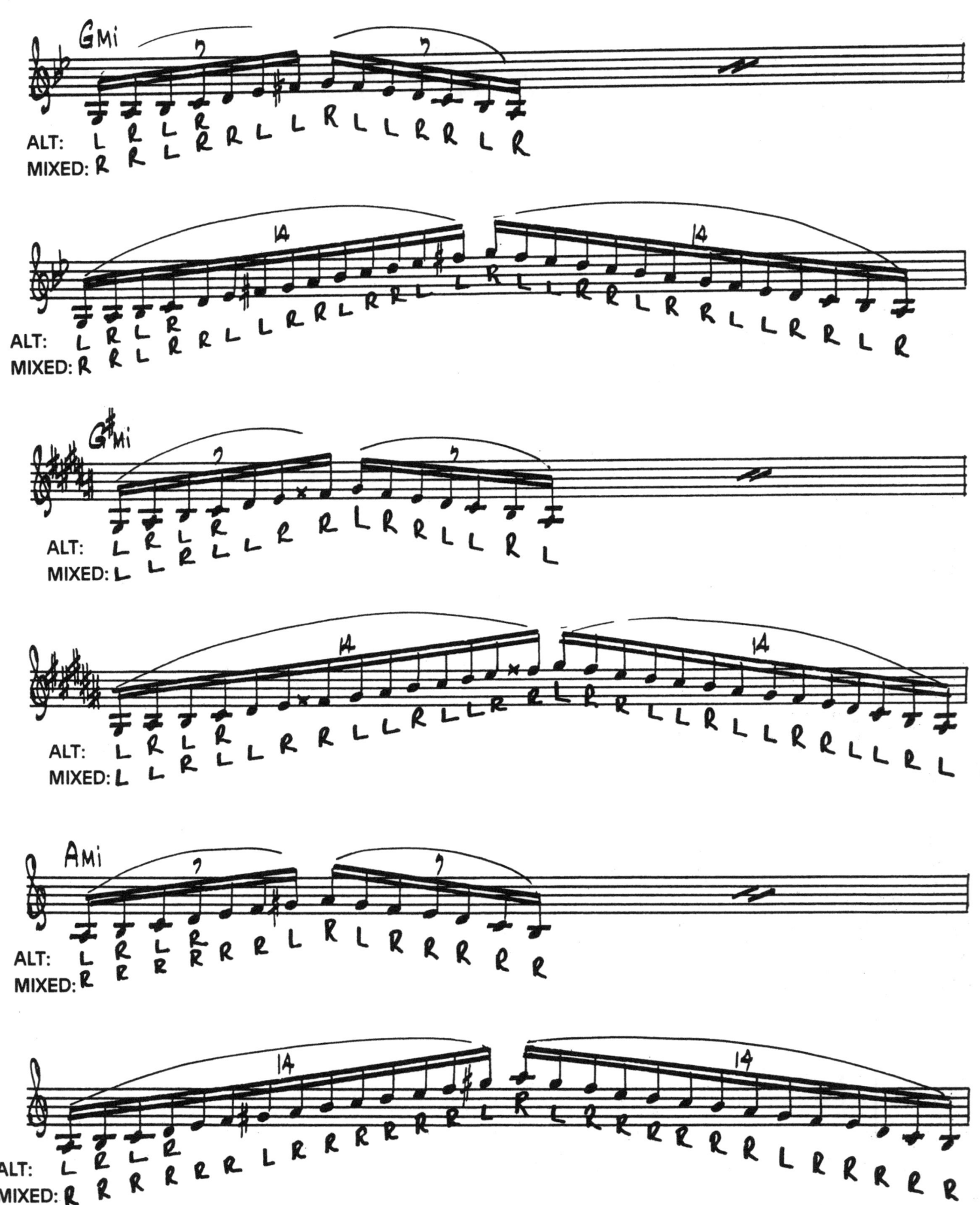

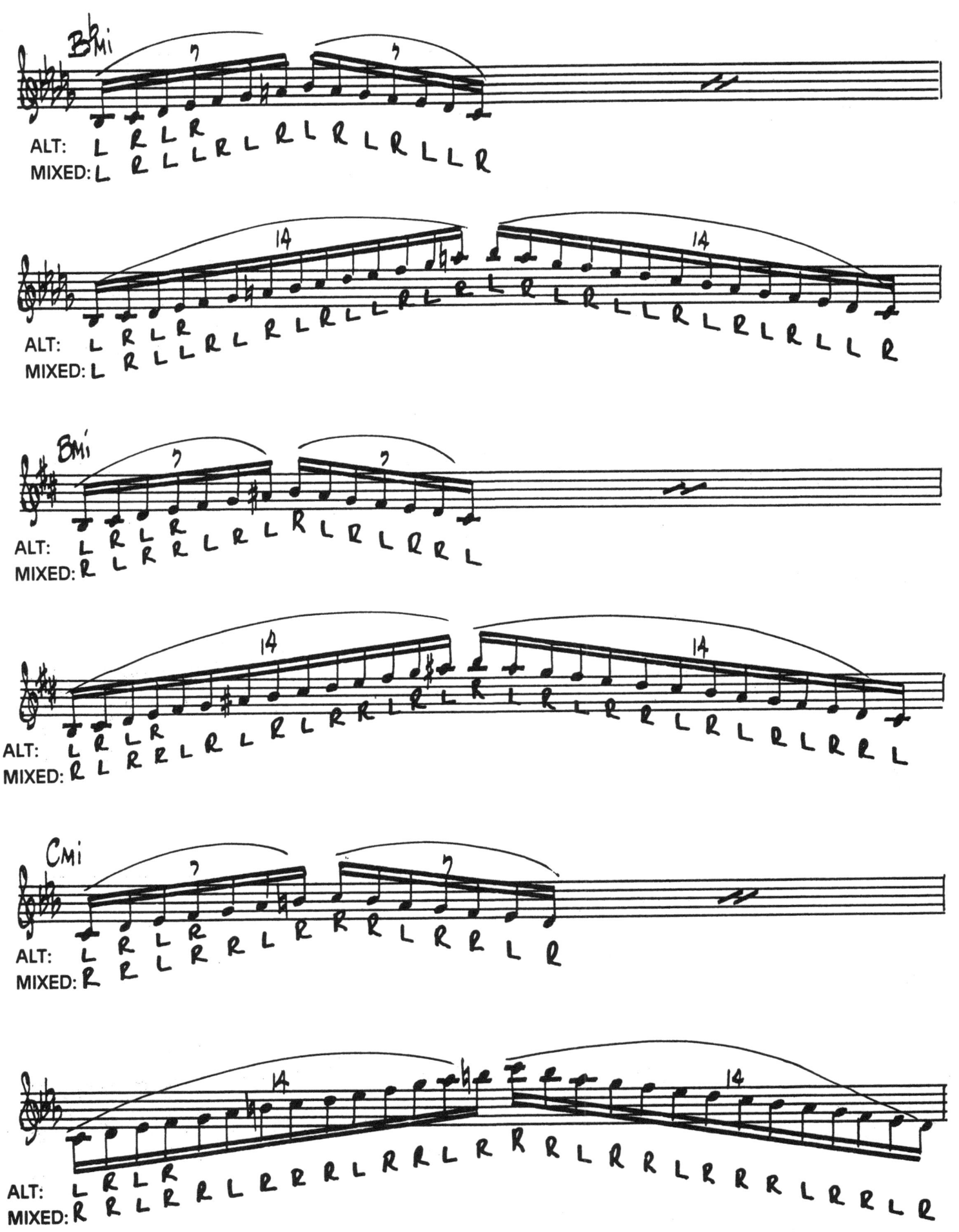

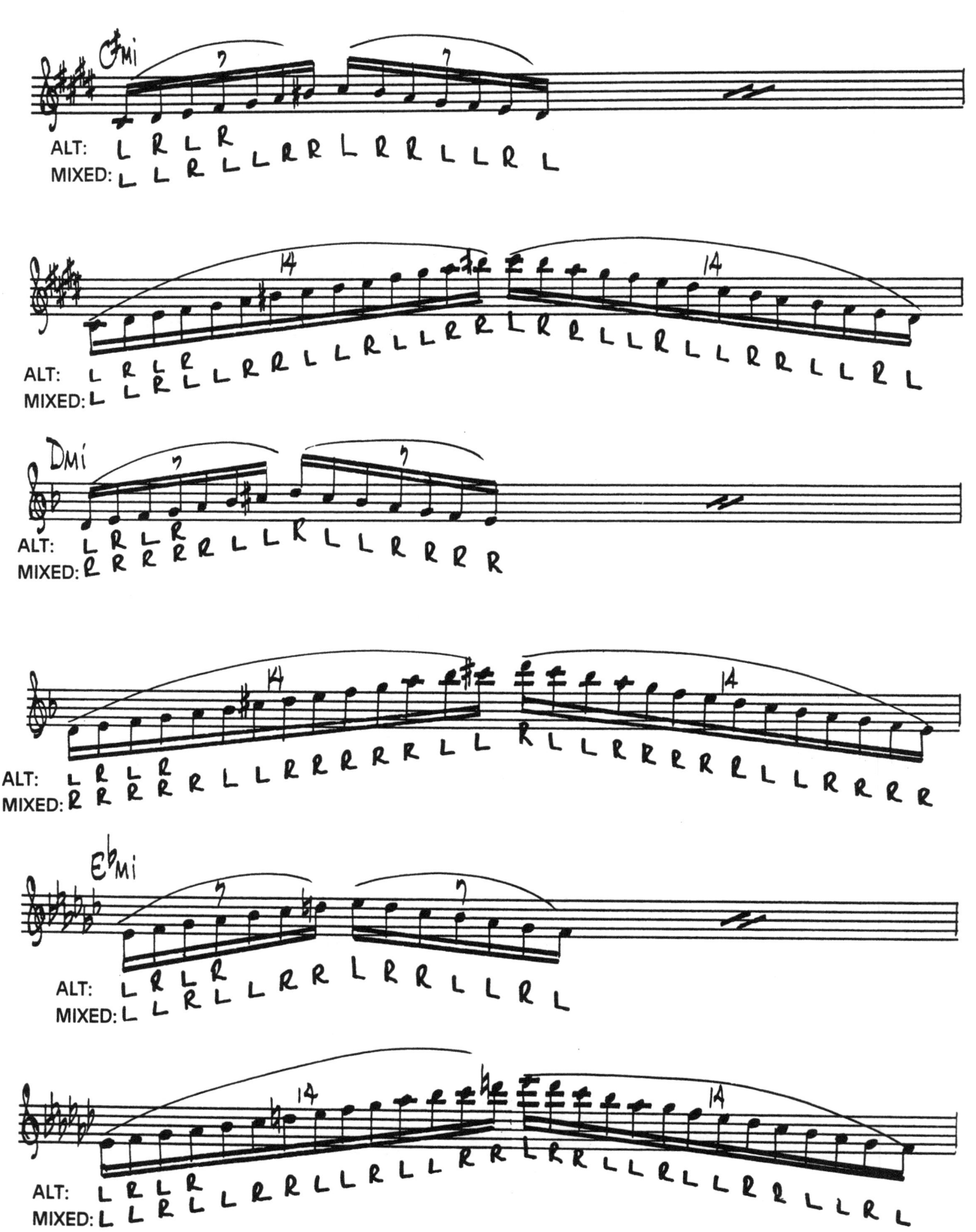

DORIAN MODES (Scales)

Play these next five pages continuously as one exercise, once they are memorized. Move on to each new scale without repeating the starting note of the preceding scale. Use alternating stickings when playing the complete exercise. After mastering pages 28 through 32 with alternating stickings, re-learn the exercise using mixed stickings.

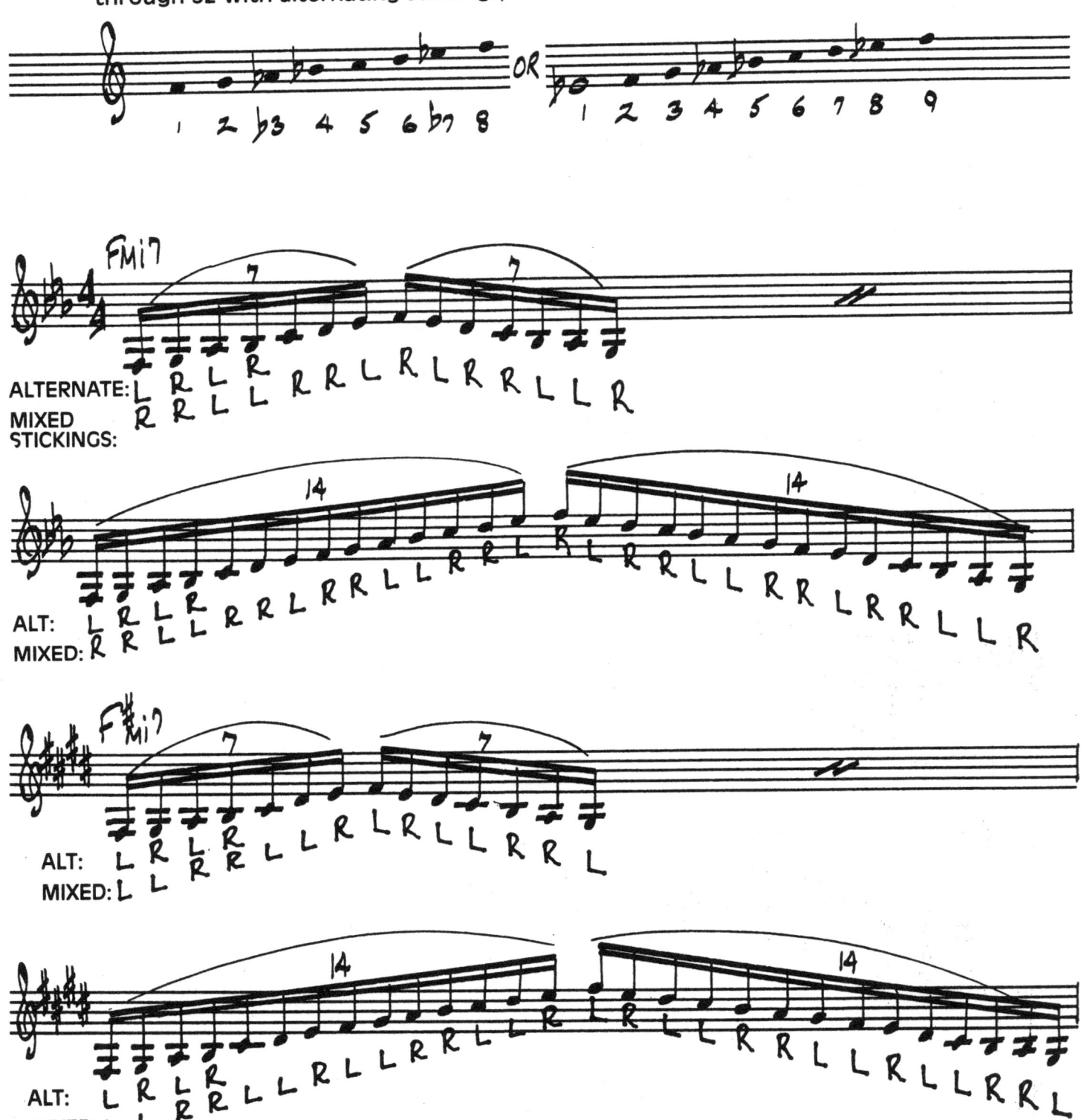

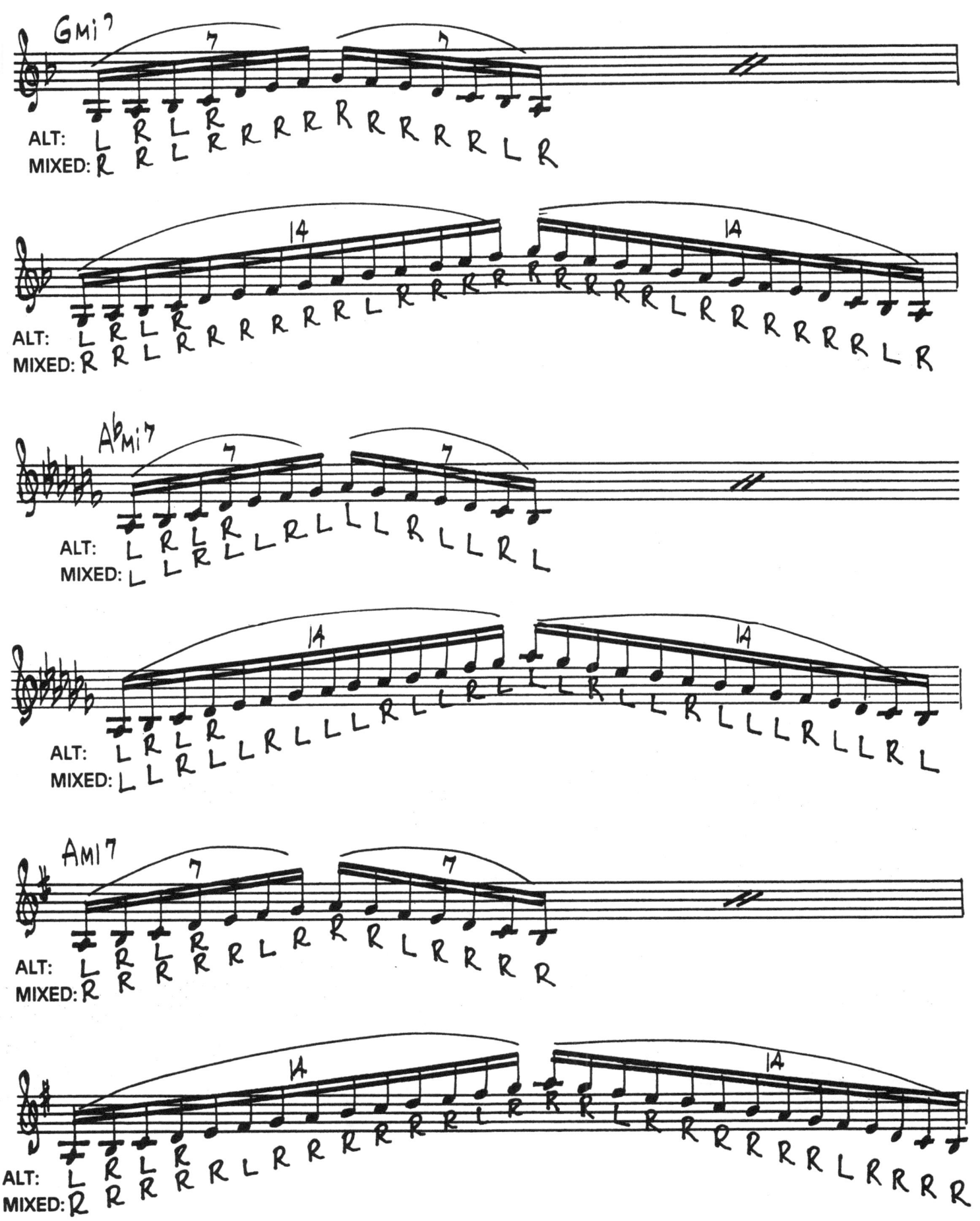

30

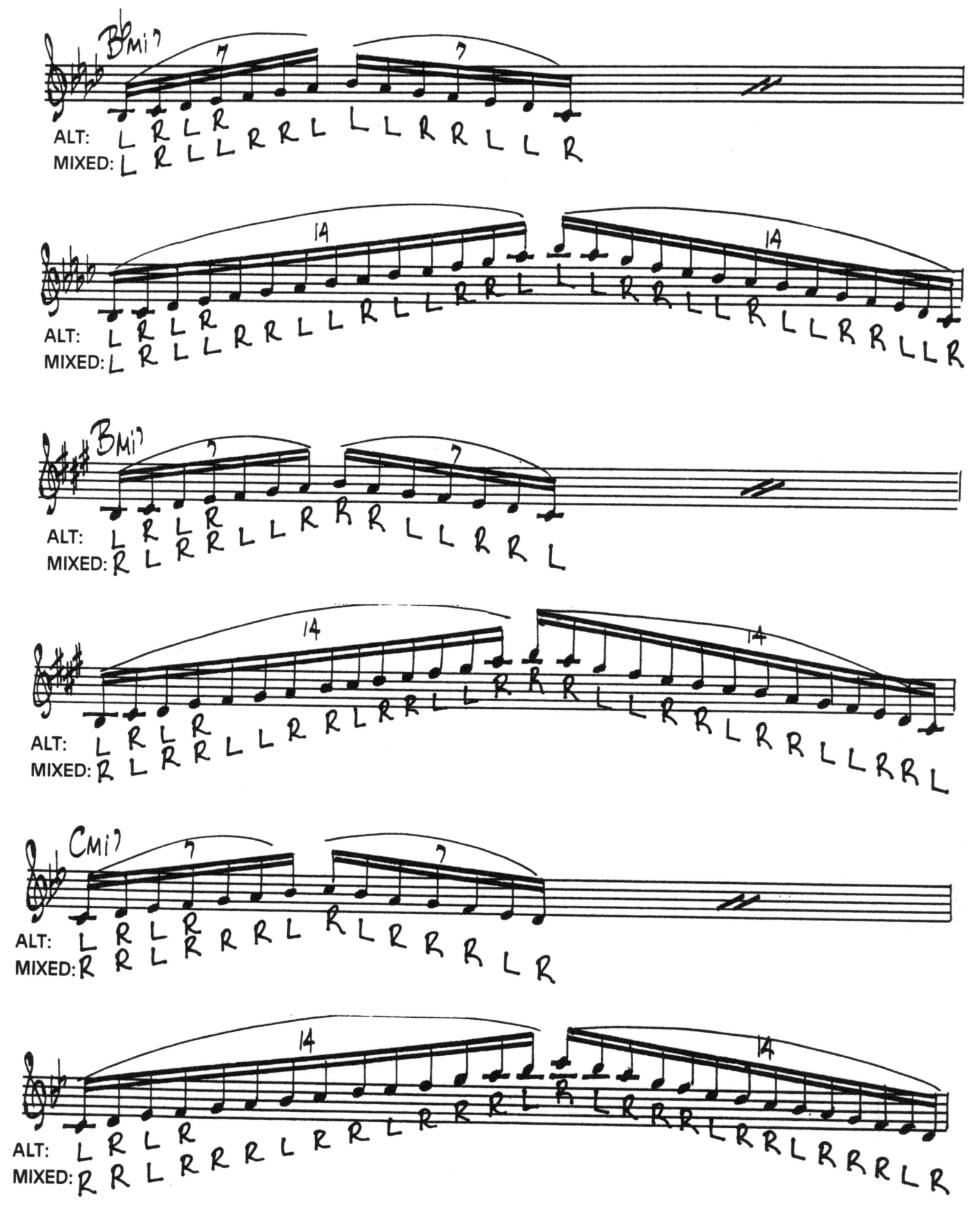

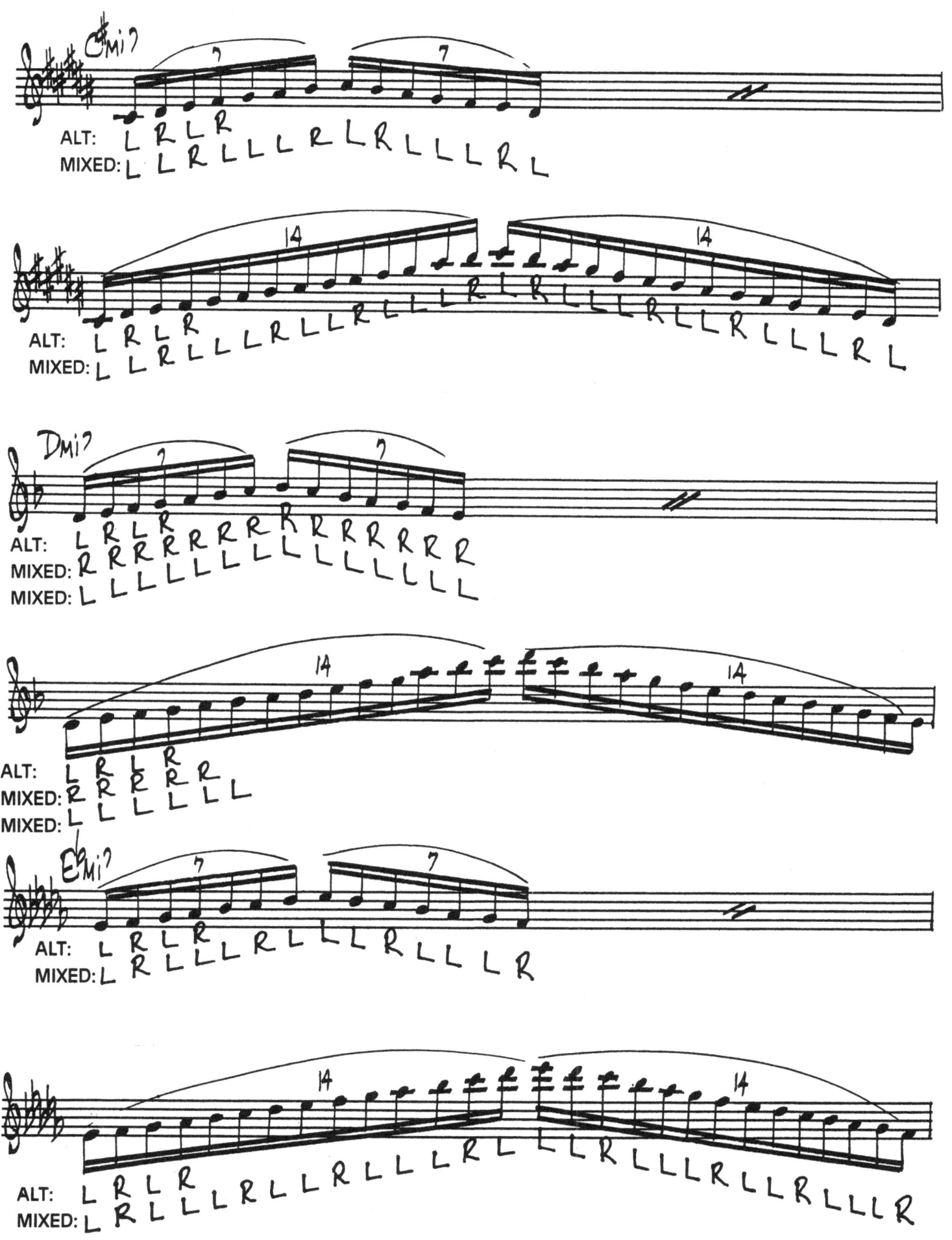

MINOR ARPEGGIOS

Play the following exercise continuously, in all keys using alternating stickings. After mastering it with alternating stickings, re-learn the exercise using mixed stickings.

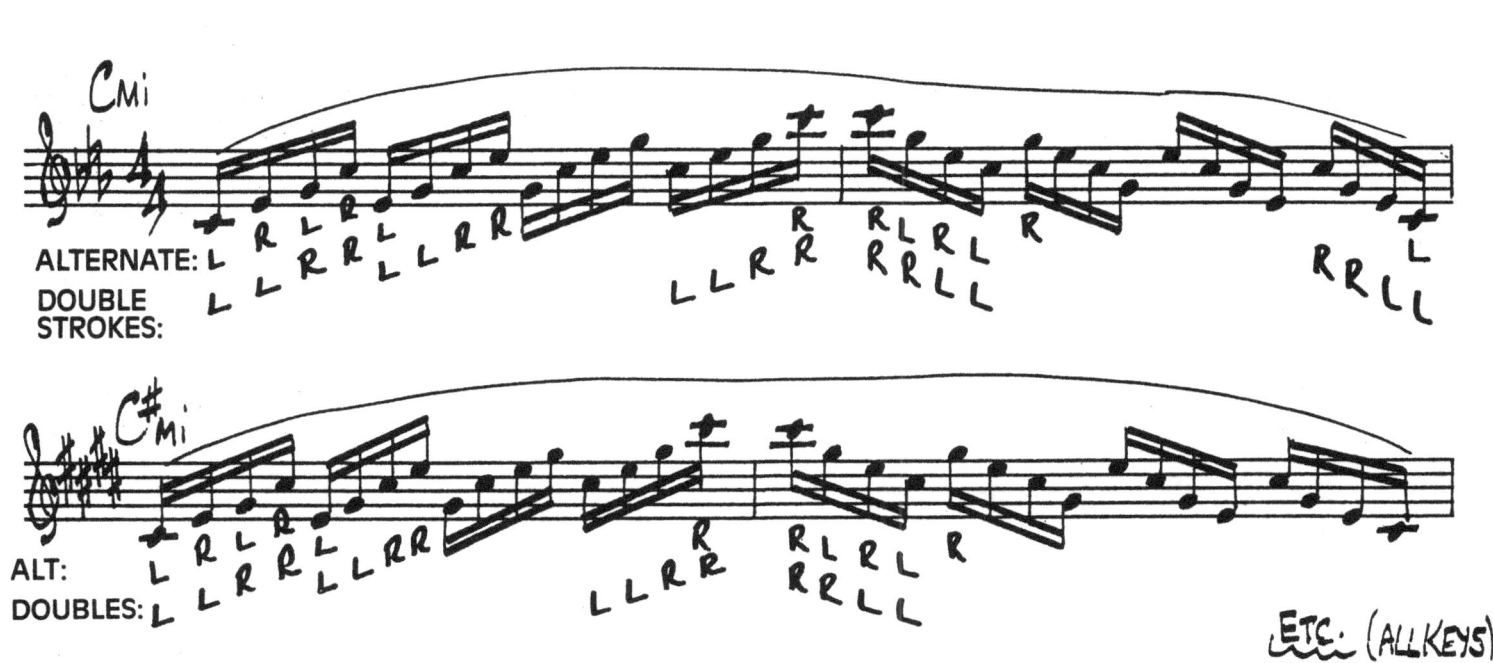

MINOR ARPEGGIOS (Reversed)

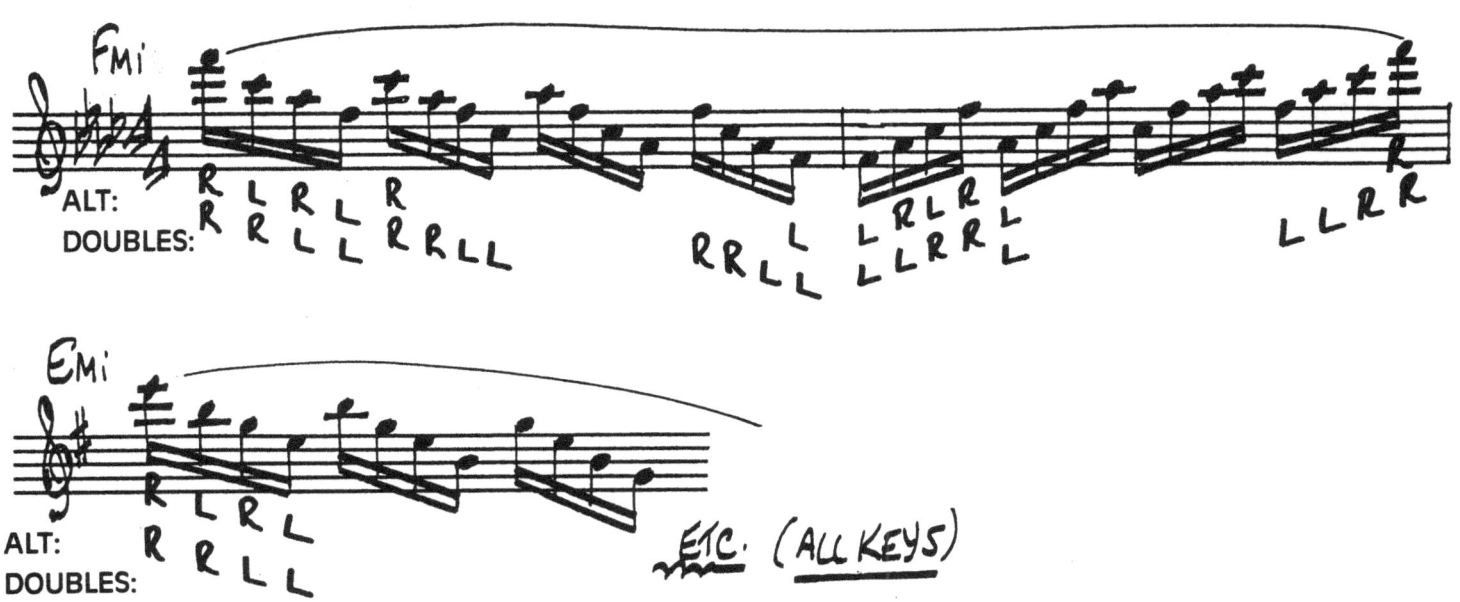

MINOR SEVENTH ARPEGGIOS

Play the following exercise continuously, in all keys using alternating stickings. After mastering it with alternating stickings, re-learn the exercise using mixed stickings.

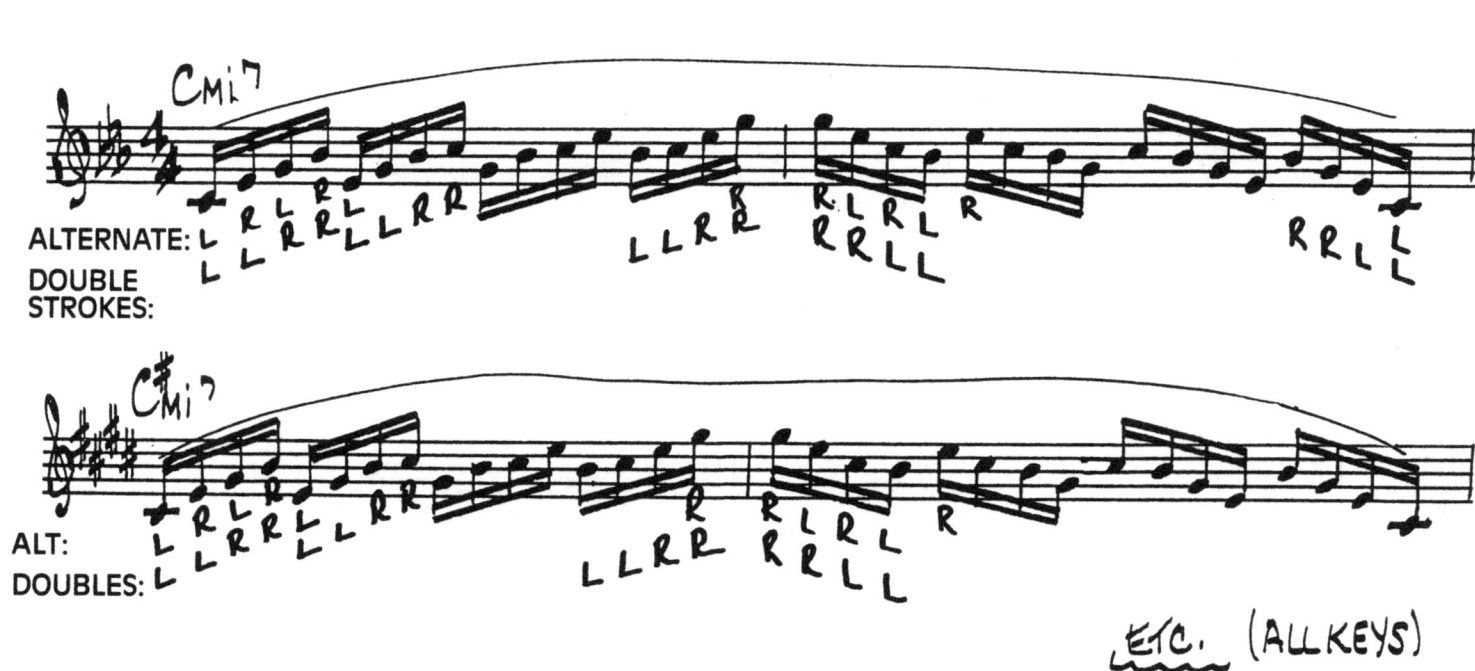

MINOR SEVENTH ARPEGGIOS (Reversed)

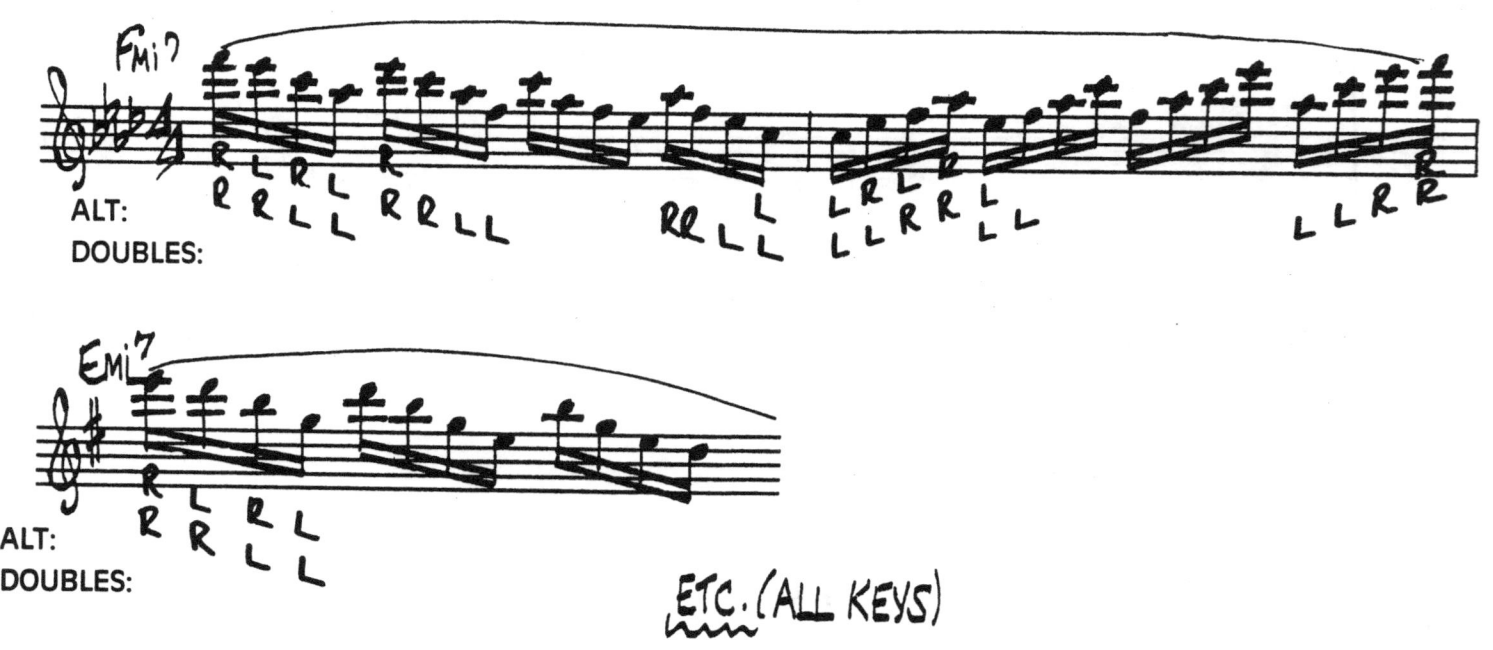

MINOR ELEVENTH ARPEGGIOS

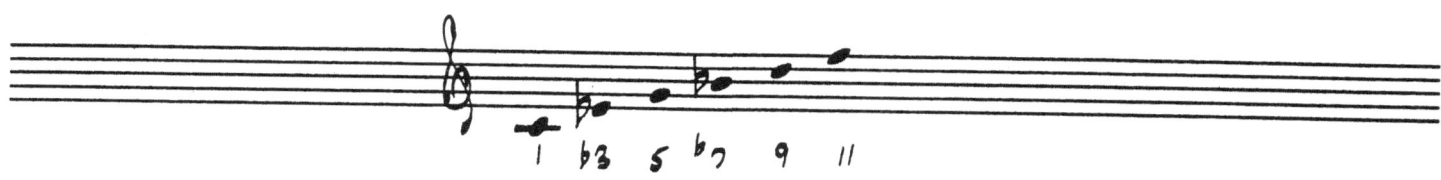

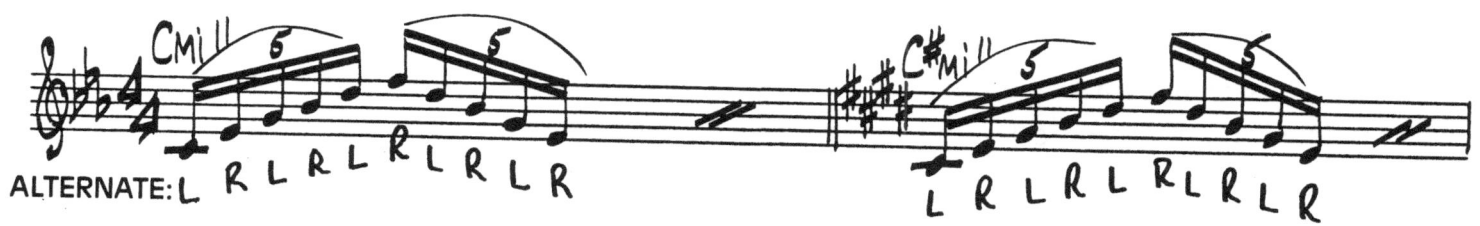

ETC. (ALL KEYS)

"CREATIVE" SCALE PRACTICE:
A "COMMON NOTE" SCALE EXERCISE AND OTHERS

Once the notes have been mastered, playing scales can become dull and seems to stifle creativity. Since playing solos on chord progressions requires one to **think ahead**, often at very fast tempos, the "COMMON NOTE" SCALE EXERCISE is used as a warmup vehicle by many jazz performers. This exercise is exciting because it requires one to think ahead harmonically as well as technically, resulting in a more practical (and music-like) "brain teaser" warm-up.

Look at the exercise to the right on the following page. We have arbitrarily chosen to start on a low C on the instrument and decided to warm up with five commonly used jazz scales: Major scale, Mixolydian mode, Dorian mode, Harmonic minor scale and Blues scale. Keeping that same scale order we run a two octave scale in each of those five tonalities from our C starting note. Once you have finishd playing all five tonalities from the low C, move up ½ step and do the same sequence from D♭. Continue this sequence until you have used all twelve chromatic notes as starting points. Be sure to start at the lowest note on your vibraphone or marimba rather than as it is printed here. Continue this "common note" exercise all the way up the instrument.

Once one has mastered the "common note" exercise at a steady and fast tempo, choose different scales than those mentioned. For instance, one might start the exercise on a very low F and begin with pentatonics, then diminished scale, then dominant scale, then arpeggiated chords, etc. Each day one can develop bigger ears and more creativity by changing the sequence of the scales used, or by practicing different, more "outside" tonalities or scales.

FULL RANGE SCALE PRACTICE

Another way to play scales which stimulates creativity and a larger awareness of the vibraphone is to play all the scales/modes from low F (or F♯) to high F (or E) regardless of which scale you are playing. In other words, be able to play all the scales and modes the full range of the vibraphone or marimba regardless of the tonality.

Many jazz musicians also practice "running changes" the full range of the instrument. For example, take a tune on which you wish to solo and play the proper scale or mode instead of the chord. Keep eighth notes in 4/4 time and start on the lowest note of the instrument. When you get to the second measure and start the next mode or scale, **don't** start each scale from the bottom, but continue up and down the instrument "running the changes". There are hundreds of ways to make scale practice creative, musical and continually stimulating. Warming up with another player's exercise is also fun and stimulates ear playing.

A "COMMON NOTE" SCALE EXERCISE

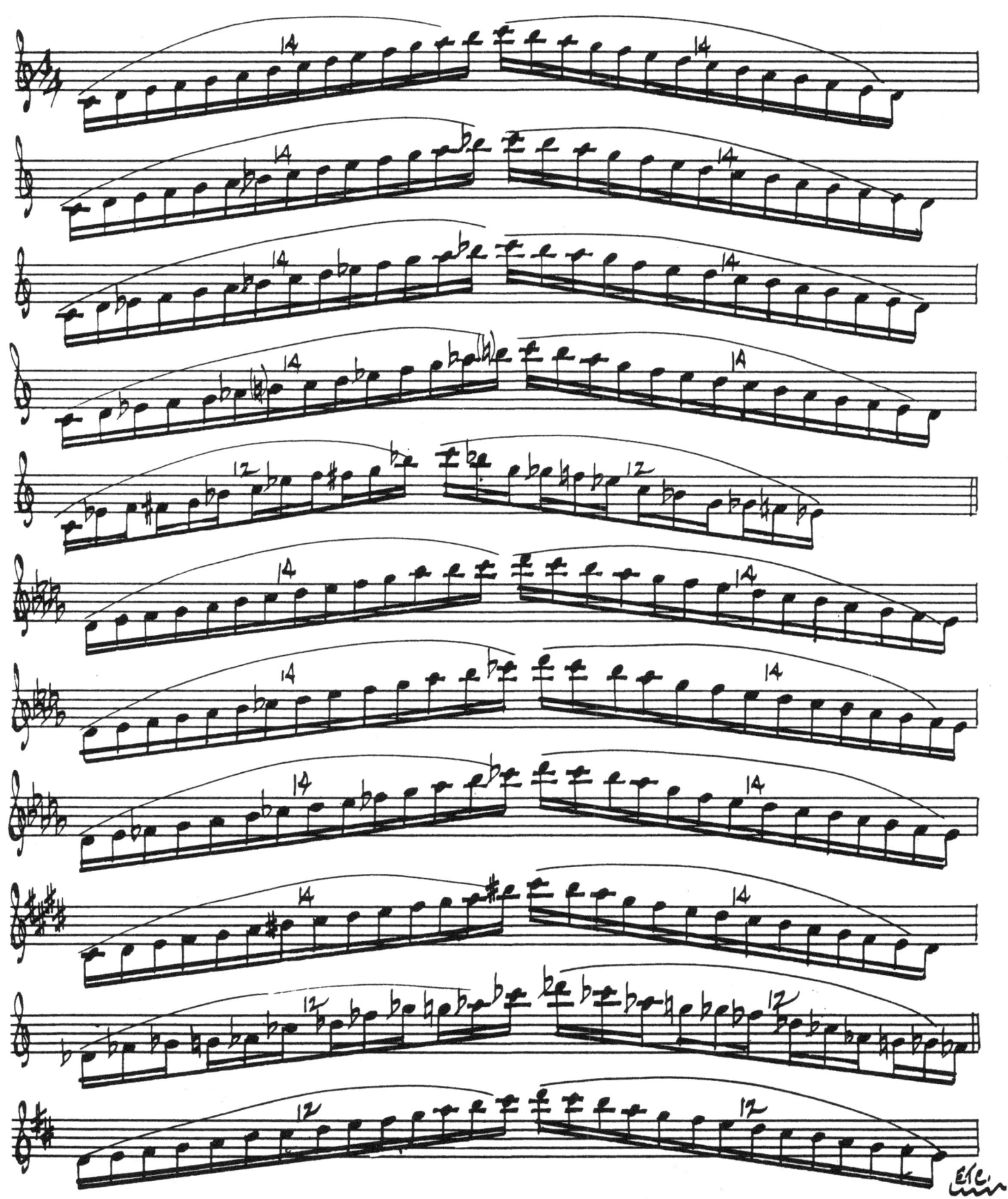

DIMINISHED SEVENTH ARPEGGIOS

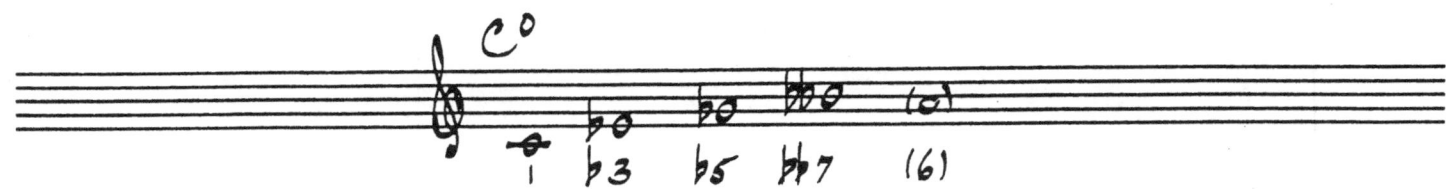

ALTERNATE:

ALT:

REVERSED

ALT:

THE DIMINISHED SCALE ("Whole Step-Half Step" Scale)

NOTE: E flat diminished seven is the SAME enharmonically as C diminished seven. That is, there are simply THREE diminished seventh chords. While they can be written differently (enharmonically), you only have to learn THREE scales. There are just THREE diminished seven scale patterns; also only three dimished seventh chords (enharmonically spelled).

C diminished seven is the same as E flat diminished seven which is the same as F sharp diminished seven which is the same as A diminished seven. C sharp diminished seven is the same as E diminished seven which is the same as G diminished seven which is the same as B flat diminished seven. D diminished seven is the same as F diminished seven which is the same as A flat diminished seven which is the same as B diminished seven. This same relationship pattern holds true in all keys, although they will be spelled differently enharmonically.

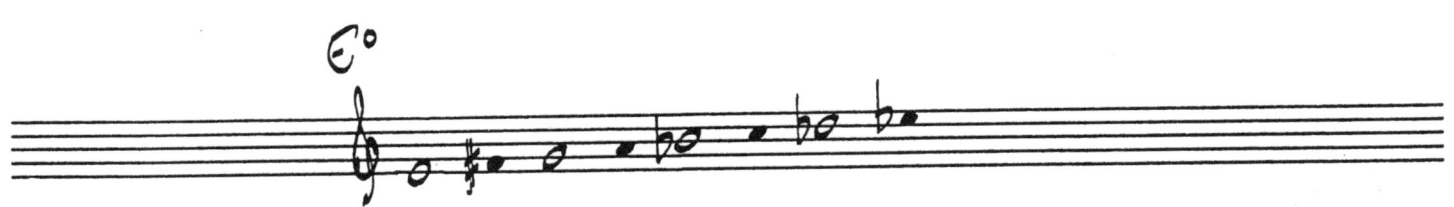

PLAY IN ALL KEYS WITHOUT STOPPING

DIMINISHED SCALE EXERCISE (Wider Range)

PLAY IN ALL KEYS WITHOUT STOPPING

THE DOMINANT SCALE ("Half Step-Whole Step" Scale)

ROOT b9 #9 3 #11 5 13 b7

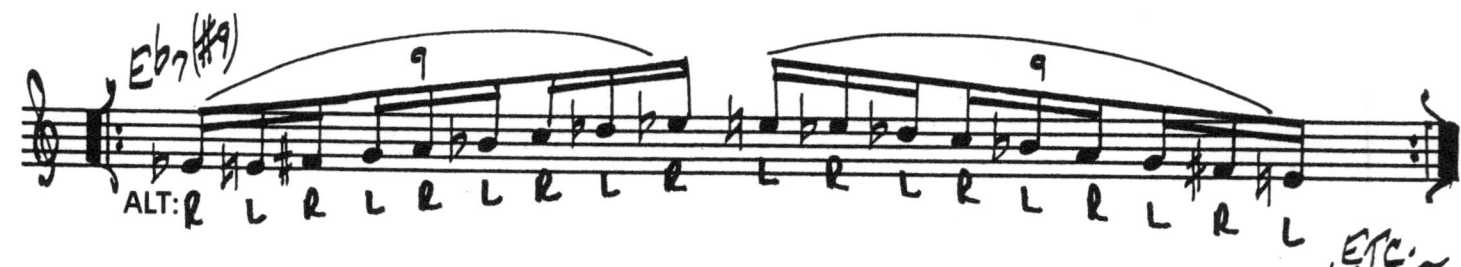

DOMINANT SCALE EXERCISE (Wider Range)

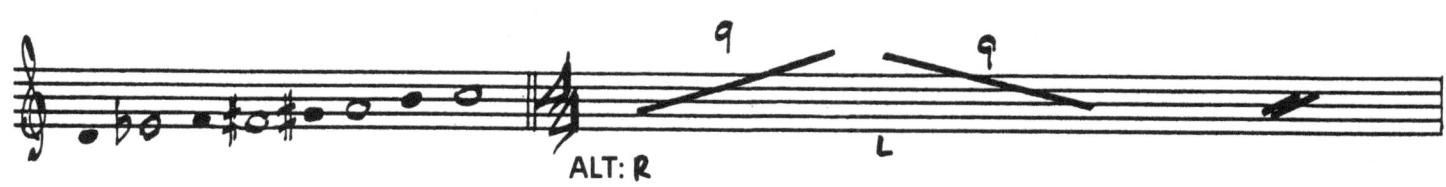

DORIAN MODE STICKING STUDY No. 1

ALTERNATE: L R L R
L L R R L L R R

DOUBLE STROKES:

ALT:
DOUBLES:
L L R R

ALT: R L R L
DOUBLES: R R L L

ETC. (PLAY IN ALL KEYS)

REVERSE IT

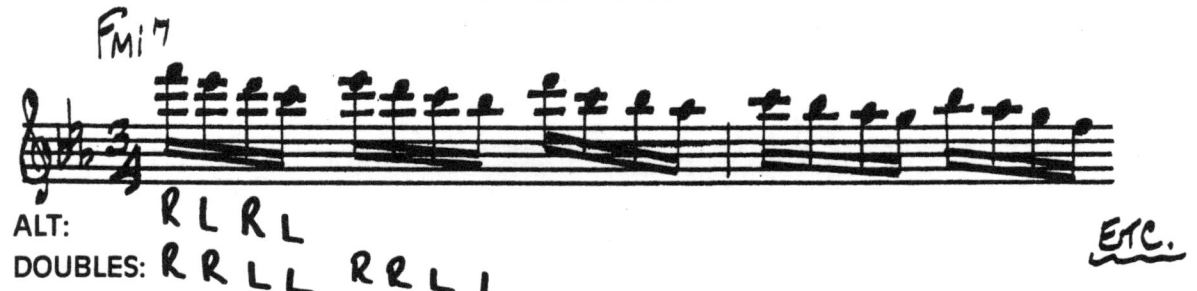

ALT: R L R L
DOUBLES: R R L L R R L L

ETC.

DORIAN MODE STICKING STUDY No. 2: "Double Strokes"

DOUBLE STROKES: L R R L L L R R L L R R L L R R L L R R L L L R R L L L R R L

DOUBLES: L R R L L L R R L L L R R L L L R R L L R R L R

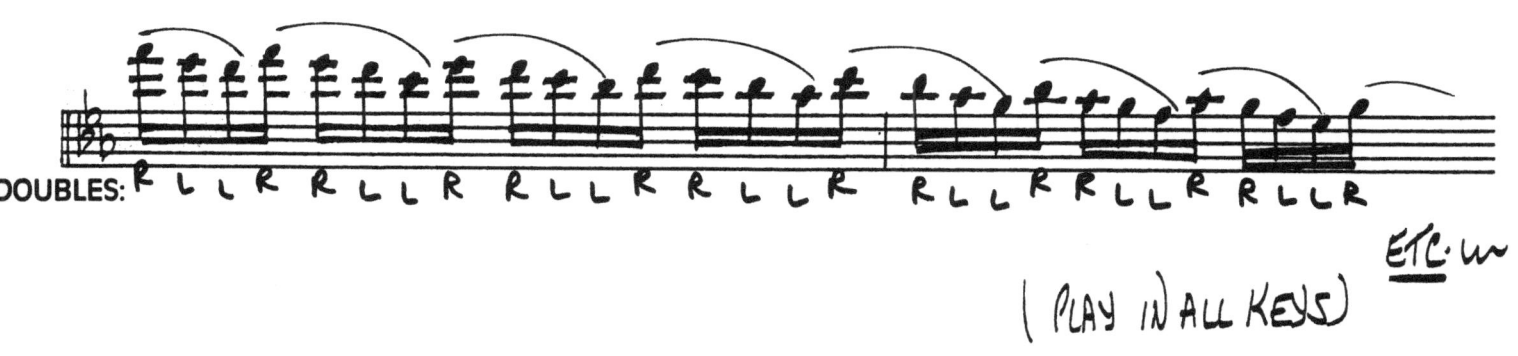

DOUBLES: R L L R L L R L L R L L R R L L R L L R R L L R R L L R R L L R

(PLAY IN ALL KEYS)

ETC.

DORIAN MODE STICKING STUDY No. 3 "Double Strokes Triads"

Continued on next page.

(PLAY IN ALL KEYS)

DORIAN MODE STICKING STUDY No. 4
"Double Strokes in Sixteenths"

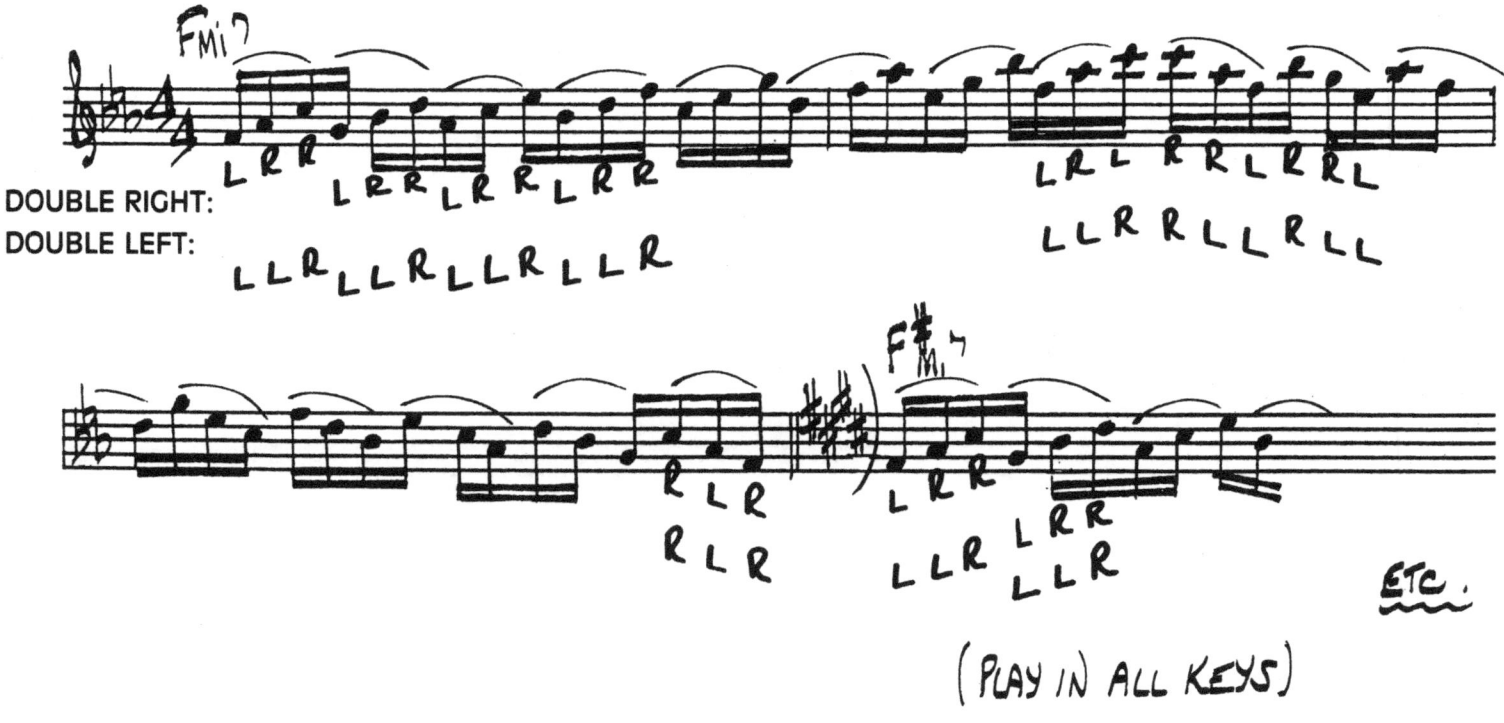

(PLAY IN ALL KEYS)

"SUS" CHORDS (Arpeggios)

ETC.   (PLAY IN ALL KEYS)

"SUS" CHORDS (Reversed)

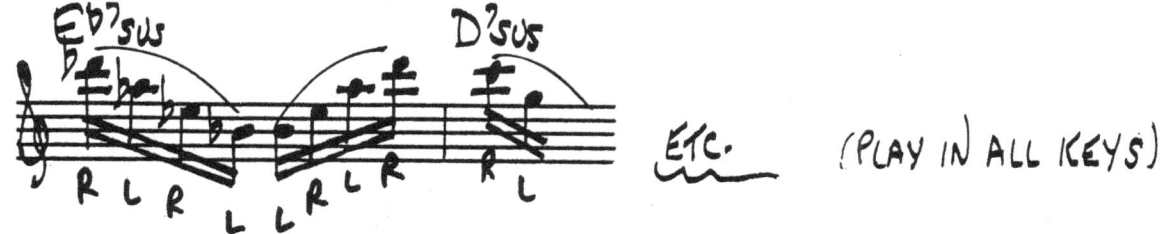

ETC.   (PLAY IN ALL KEYS)

CONSECUTIVE "SUS" CHORDS

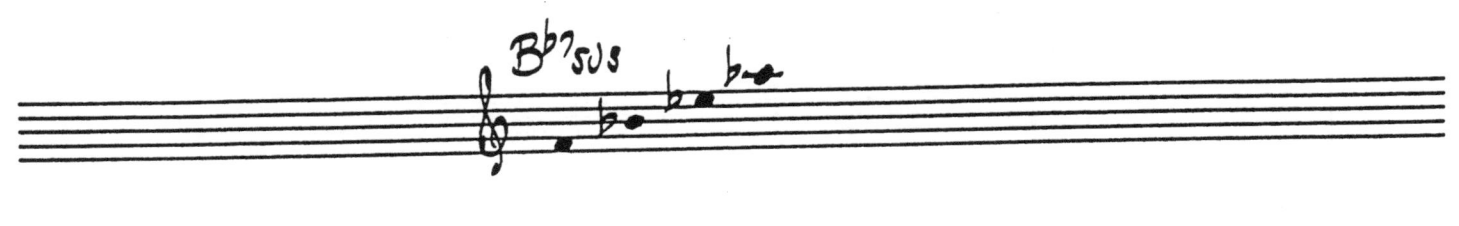

REVERSE IT

VARIATION 1

REVERSE IT

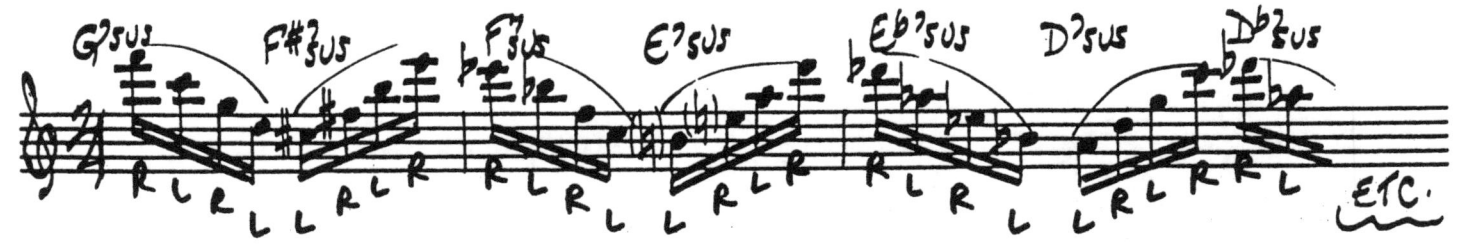

VARIATION 2

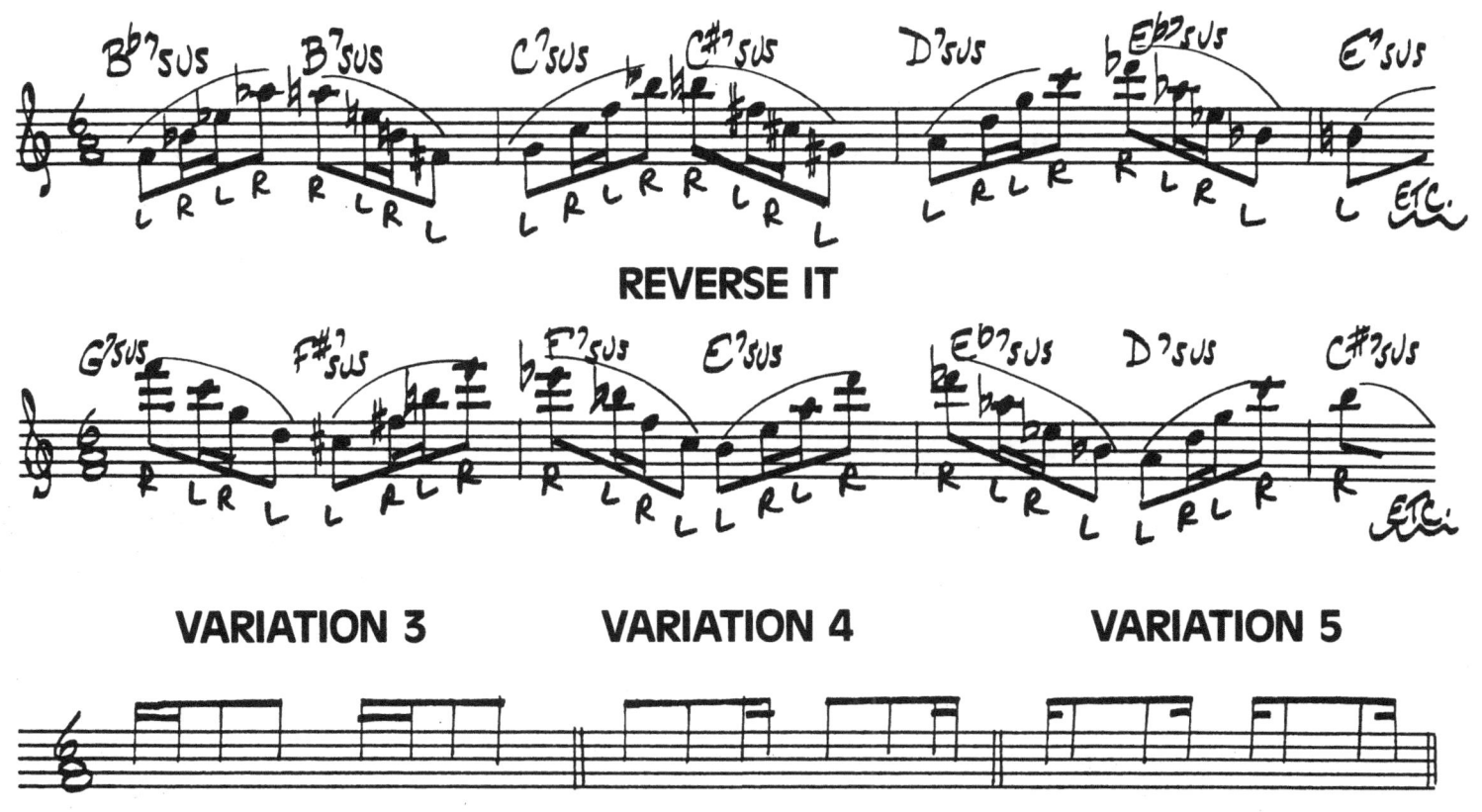

REVERSE IT

VARIATION 3   VARIATION 4   VARIATION 5

"SUS" CHORDS (Double Strokes)

DOUBLE RIGHT: L R R L R R L R R

DOUBLE LEFT: L L R L L R L L R

REVERSE IT

DOUBLE RIGHT:
DOUBLE LEFT:

PLAY FULL RANGE

PENTATONIC SCALES (Major)

ALTERNATE:
DOUBLE STROKES:

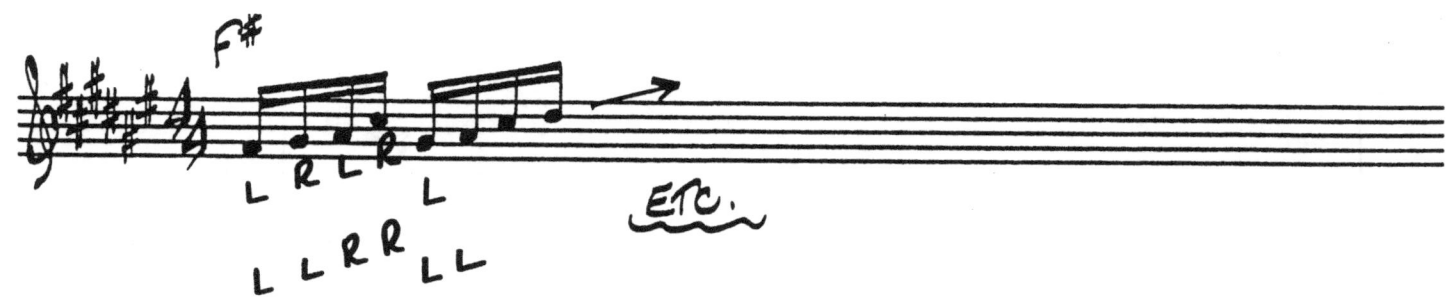

CONSECUTIVE PENTATONIC GROUPS

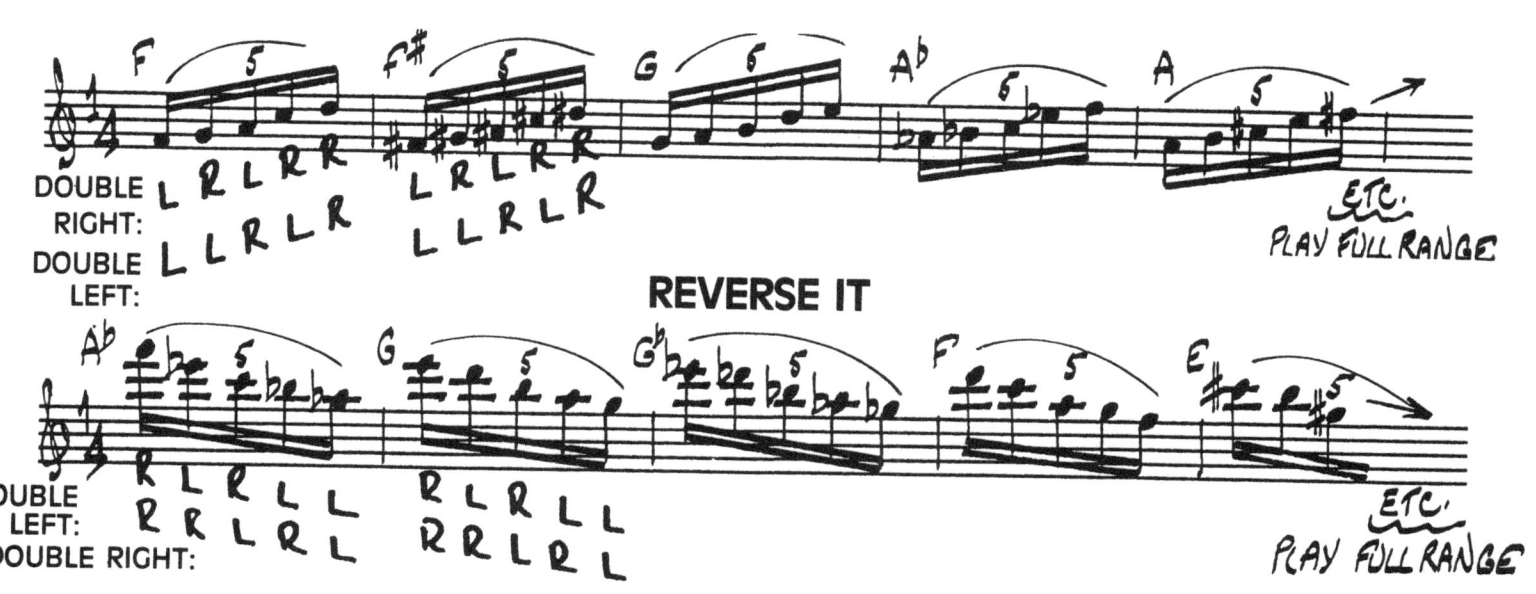

REVERSE IT

PENTATONIC SCALES (Minor)

52

ALT: L R L R L
DOUBLES: L L R R L L

ETC. PLAY FULL RANGE

CONSECUTIVE PENTATONIC GROUPS

DOUBLE
RIGHT: L L R L R L R R
DOUBLE LEFT: L L R L R L

REVERSE IT

DOUBLE LEFT: R L R L R L L
DOUBLE RIGHT: R R L R L

VARIATION 1

L R R L R L L R L R R L R L L R
R L L R L R R L R L L R L R R L

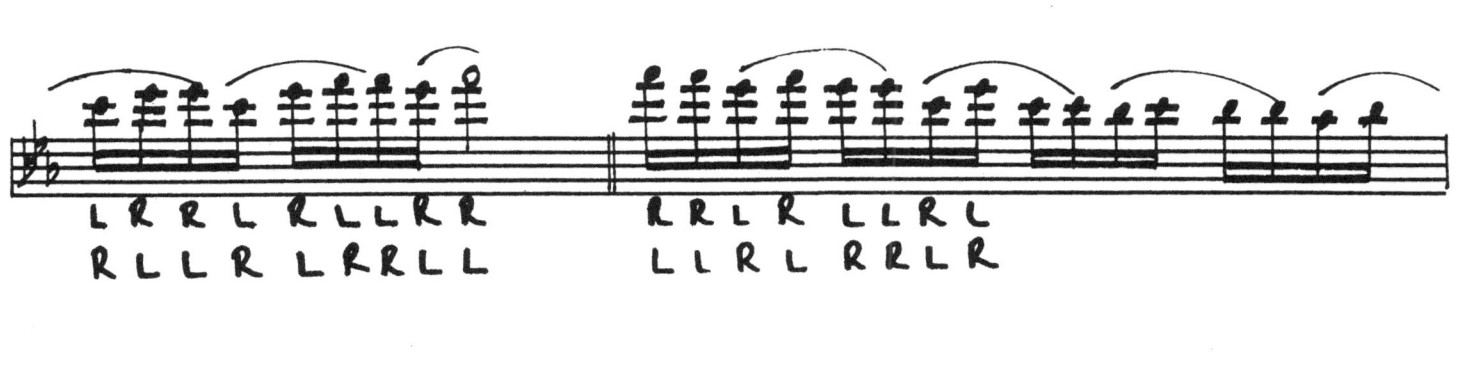

VARIATION 2

VARIATION 3

ALTERNATE: L R L R L R L R L R L R L R L R

MIXED STICKINGS: L R L L R R L R L L R R

REVERSE IT

ALT: R L R L R L R L R L R L R L

MIXED: R L R R L L R L R R L L

VARIATION 4

ALT: R L R L R L R L R L R L R L

MIXED: R L R R L L R L R R L L L

REVERSE IT

ALT: L R L R L R L R L R L R L R L R

MIXED: L R L L R R L R L R L L R R

VARIATION 5

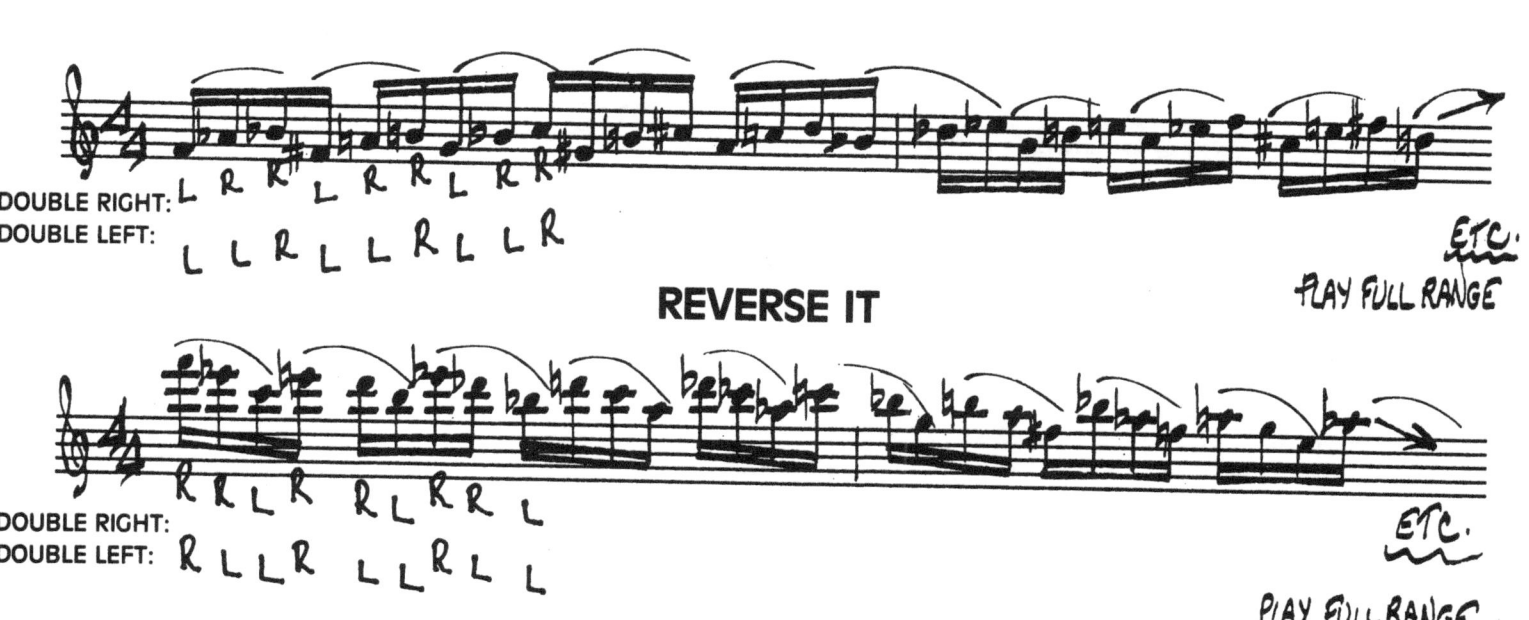

DOUBLE RIGHT: L R R L R R L R R

DOUBLE LEFT: L L R L L R L L R

ETC.
PLAY FULL RANGE

REVERSE IT

DOUBLE RIGHT: R R L R R L R R L

DOUBLE LEFT: R L L R L L R L L

ETC.
PLAY FULL RANGE

VARIATION 6

DOUBLE RIGHT: L R R L R R L R R

DOUBLE LEFT: L L R L L R L L R

ETC.

PLAY FULL RANGE

REVERSE IT

DOUBLE RIGHT:
DOUBLE LEFT:

PLAY FULL RANGE

MISCELLANEOUS INTERVAL STUDIES
MAJOR 2nds

ALTERNATE

PLAY FULL RANGE

REVERSE IT

ALTERNATE

MINOR 3rds

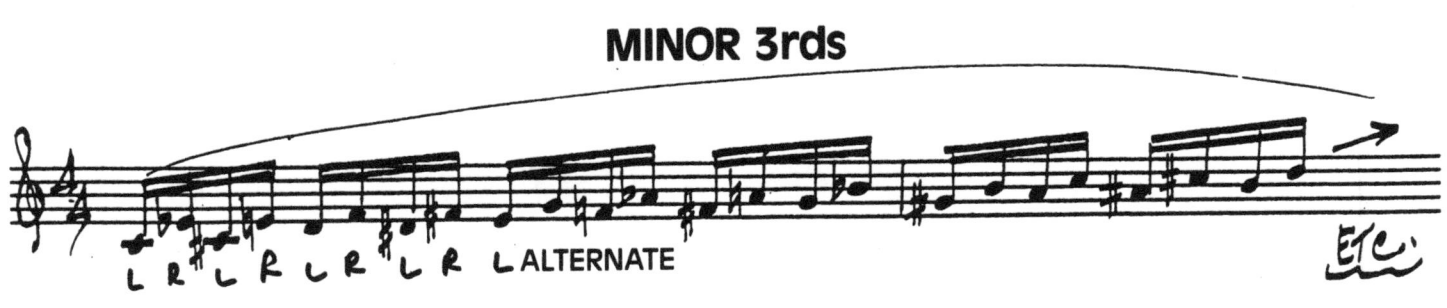

ALTERNATE

PLAY FULL RANGE

REVERSE IT

ALTERNATE

MAJOR 3rds

L R L R L R L R L ALTERNATE

ETC.
PLAY FULL RANGE

REVERSE IT

R L R L R L R L R ALTERNATE

ETC.
PLAY FULL RANGE

PERFECT 4ths

L R L R L R L R L ALTERNATE

ETC.
PLAY FULL RANGE

REVERSE IT

R L R L R L R L R ALTERNATE

ETC.
PLAY FULL RANGE

One goal of the aspiring vibist might be to acquire the pianistic, contrapuntal style of Gary Burton and David Friedman and blend it with the lyrical, vocal-like style of Milt Jackson and Bobby Hutcherson. The student vibist will therefore find thorough study necessary as the above mentioned players are consummate artists in their own right, who have spent a lifetime of work and experimentation to develop their own modern style of playing.

Musically, the player should play from a collection of jazz tunes such as can be found in the east coast fake book entitled **The Real Book.** The Jamey Aebersold jazz improvisation records also offer a "play along" system of learning tunes. Modern trends, however, require looking at the chords and chords voicings found in Ron Delp's book **Vibraphone Technique: Four Mallet Chord Voicing** (Berklee Press). From a purely technical standpoint, good hand positions and efficient technique can be achieved by playing through and mastering Gary Burton's **Four Mallet Studies,** (Universal). Those two books will assist developing a style in the "pianistic approach" to vibes playing. The vocal or lyrical style can be developed mostly by listening, transcribing and immitating Milt Jackson and Bobby Hutcherson solos off records. The art of pedal and mallet damping can be studied by playing David Friedman's **Vibraphone Technique: Mallet Pedaling and Damping** (Berklee Press). A thorough study of jazz improvisation can be achieved through a number of ways, but one interesting approach to mastering jazz vibes can be achieved by playing through Ramon Ricker's three treatese: **New Concepts in Linear Improvisation, Pentatonic Scales for Jazz Improvisation** and **Technique Development In Fourths for Jazz Improvisation** (Studio Pr) and other such books. The student should beware that the music industry has so many records and books on the market, that a careful choice must be made as to **which** books to play through and **which** players to emulate. The above methods will cover the basics necessary to play musically: improvisation, reading, memorization, comping, contrapuntal technical facility, relaxed, fluent four mallet technique, pedaling and damping, and of course listening with "big ears".

MAJOR SEVENTH CHORDS (Arpeggios)

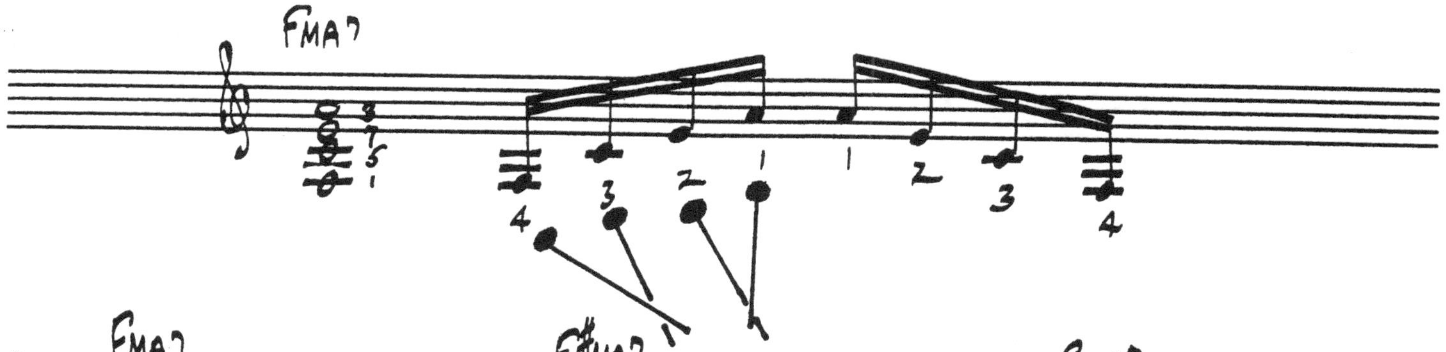

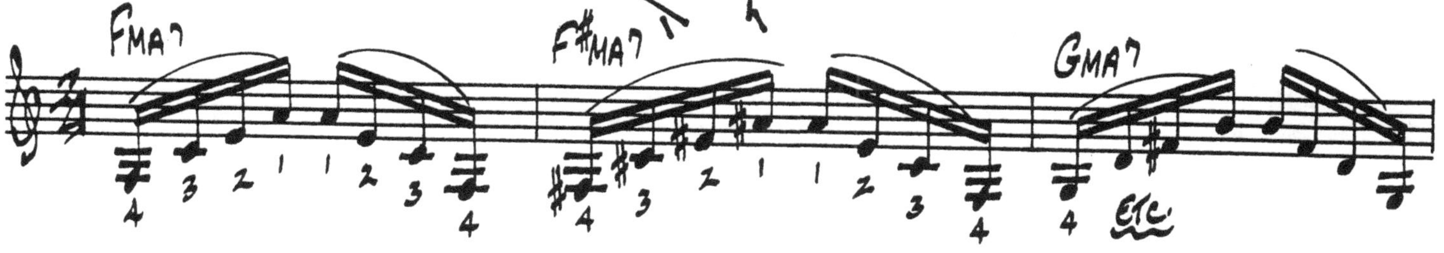

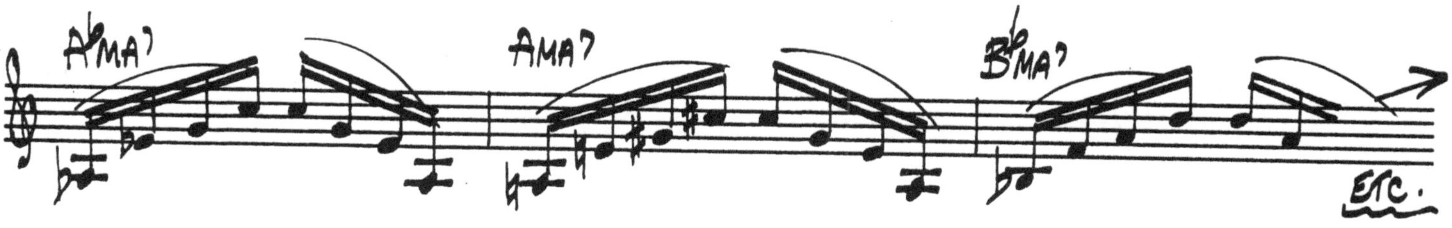

PLAY IN ALL KEYS

REVERSE IT

PLAY IN ALL KEYS

MAJOR SIXTH CHORDS

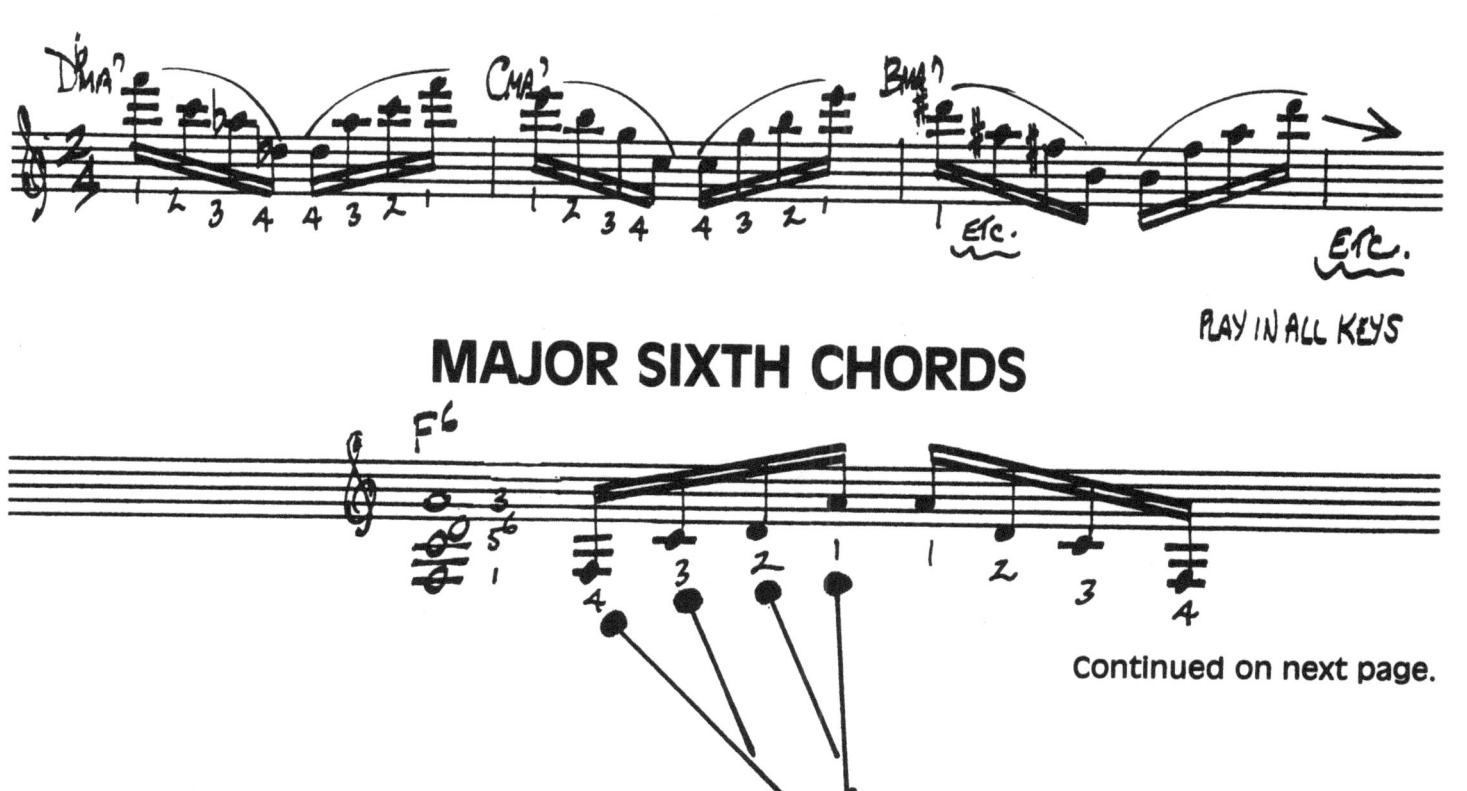

Continued on next page.

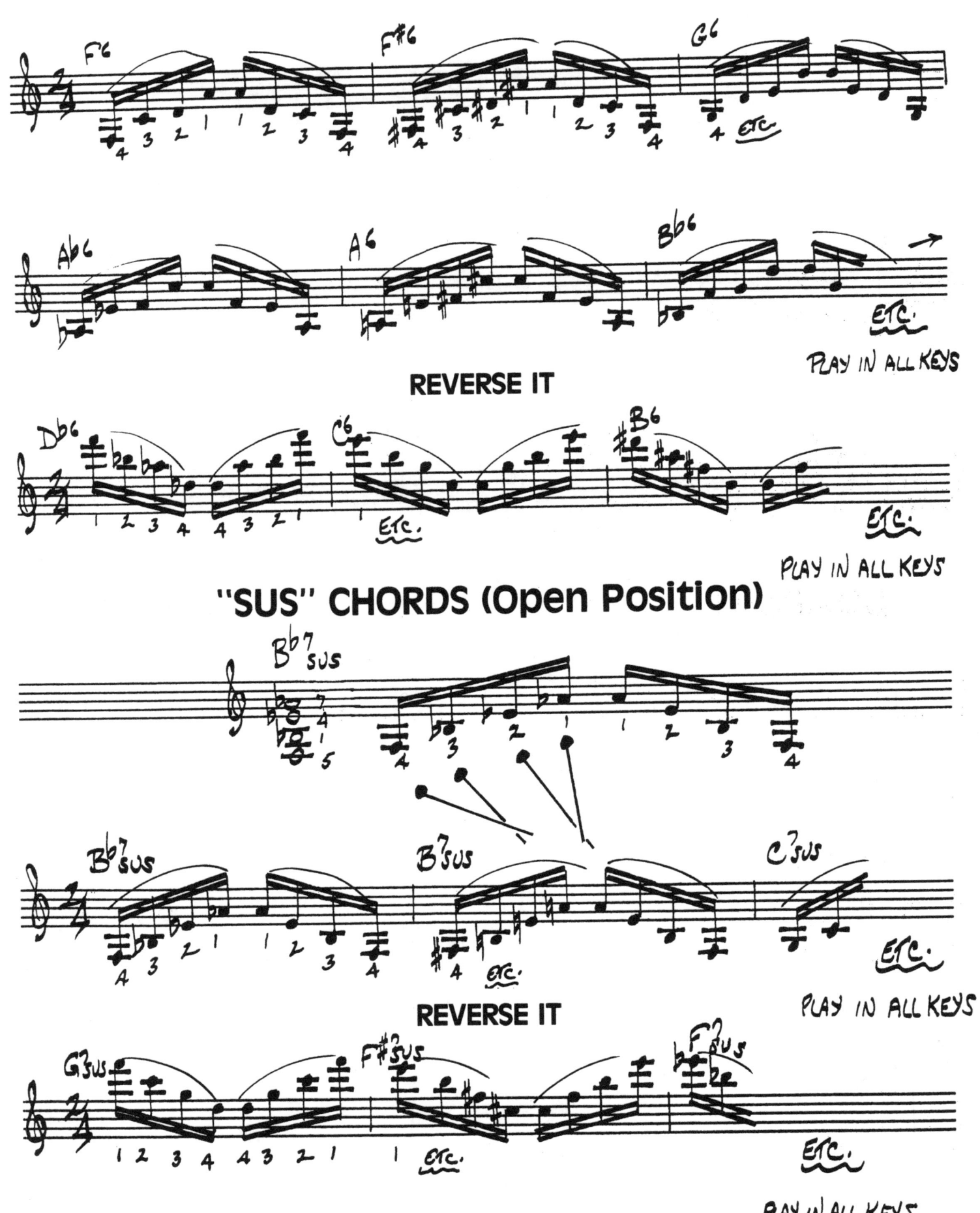

REVERSE IT

PLAY IN ALL KEYS

PLAY IN ALL KEYS

"SUS" CHORDS (Open Position)

REVERSE IT

PLAY IN ALL KEYS

PLAY IN ALL KEYS

"SUS" CHORDS (Closed Position)

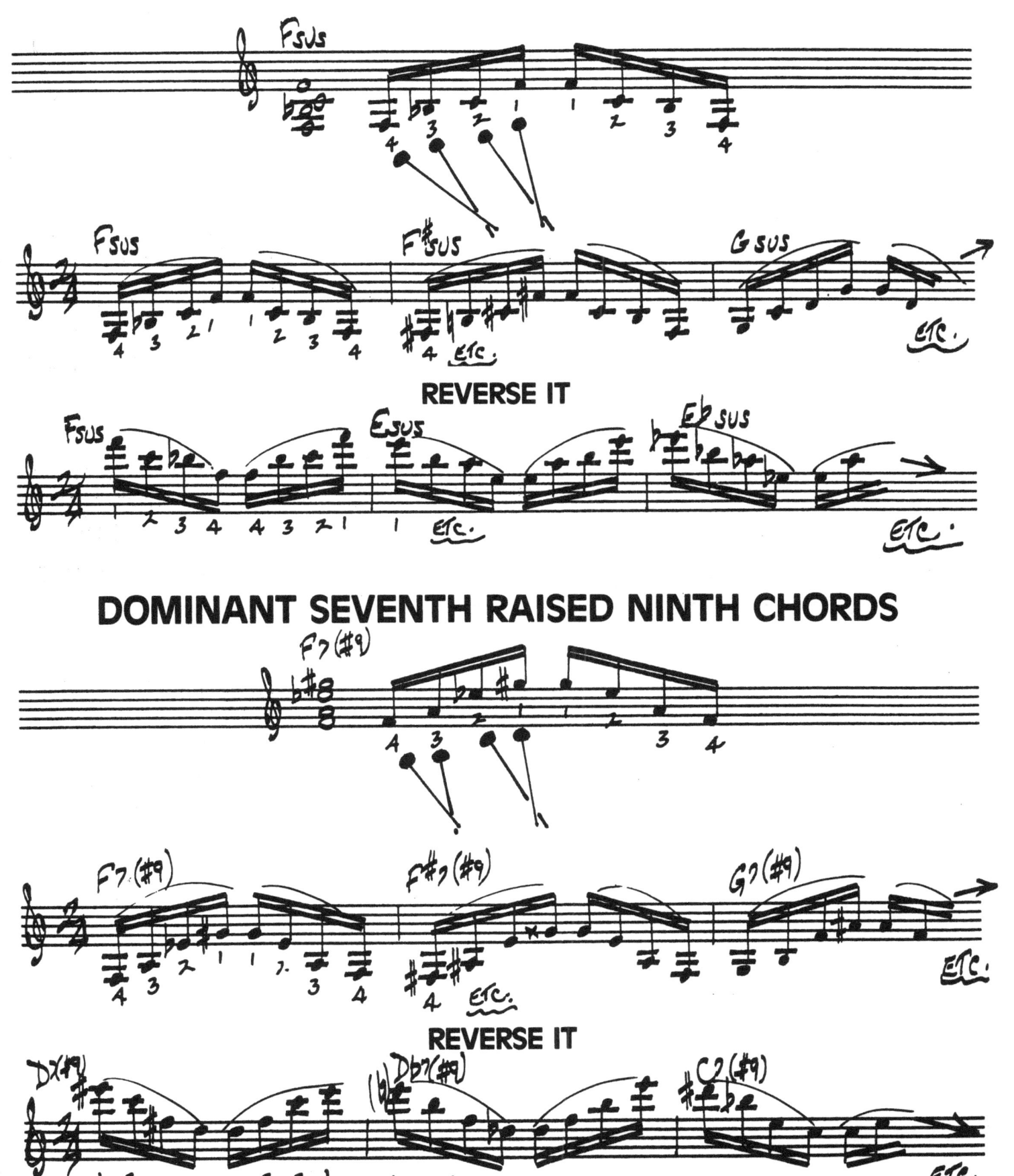

DOMINANT SEVENTH RAISED NINTH CHORDS

TWO SEVEN-FIVE SEVEN (ii7 v7) SEQUENCES

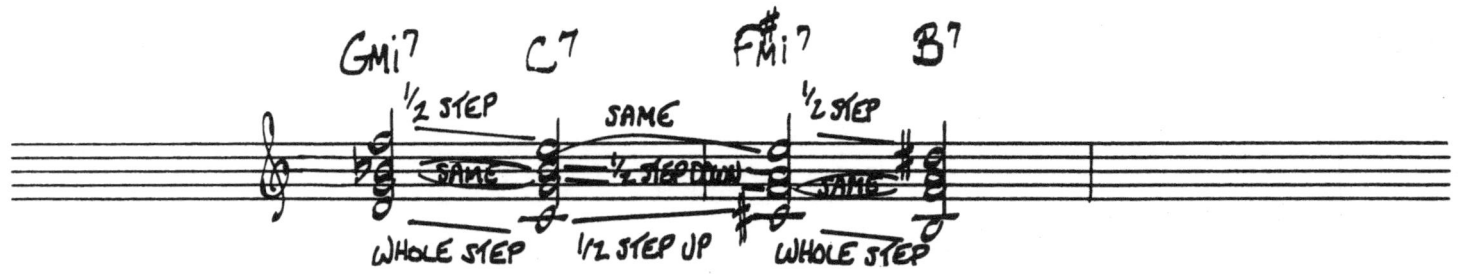

COUNTERPOINT EXERCISES

CONTRARY MOTION

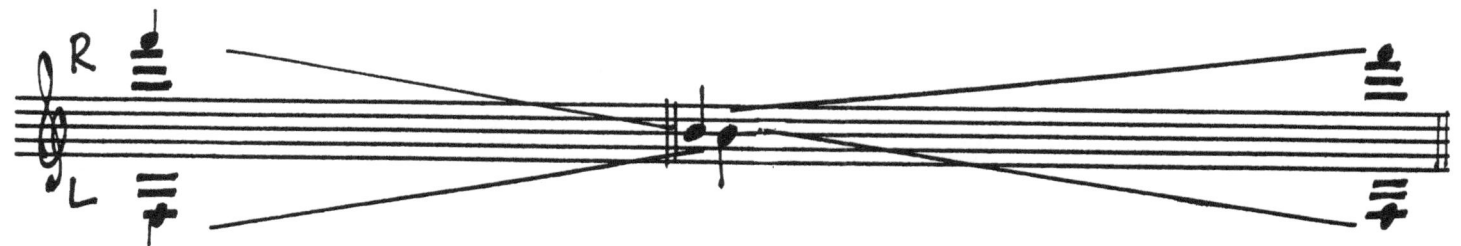

REVERSE IT

64

RIGHT HAND MELODY

REVERSE IT

LEFT HAND MELODY   REVERSE IT

VARIATION 1

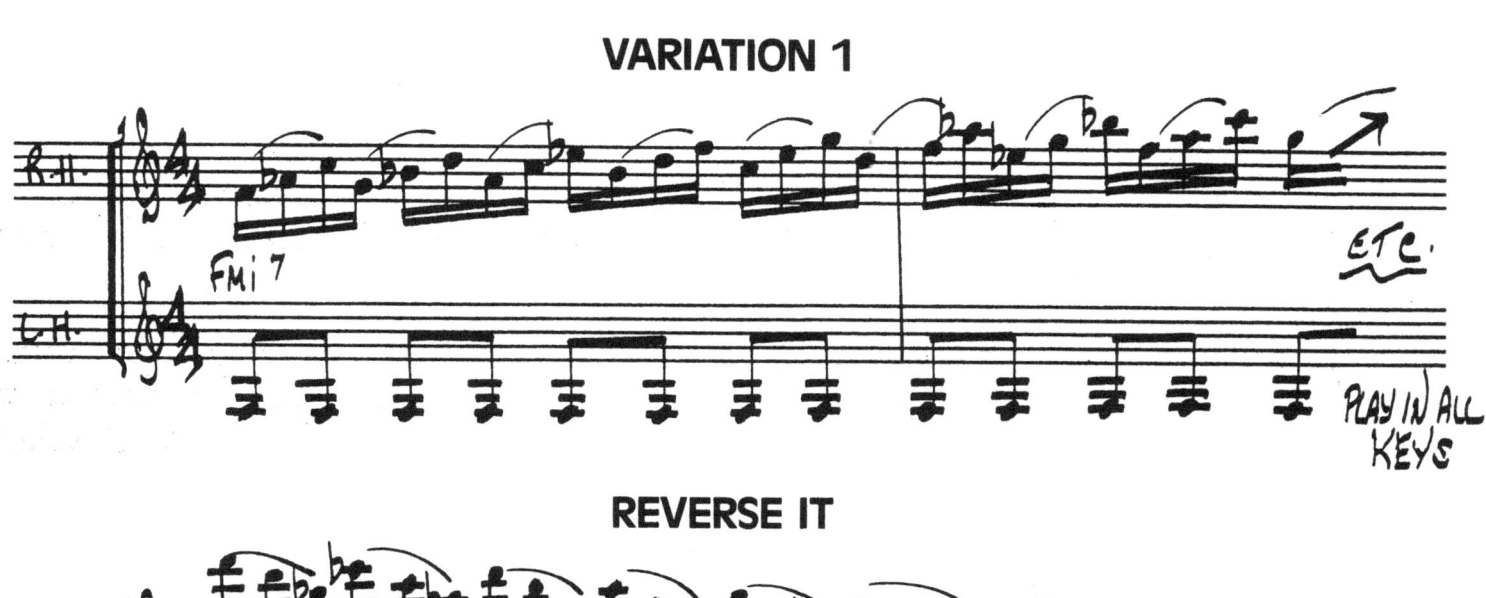

REVERSE IT

VARIATION 2

REVERSE IT

VARIATION 3 (R.H. Melody)

VARIATION 3 (L.H. Melody)

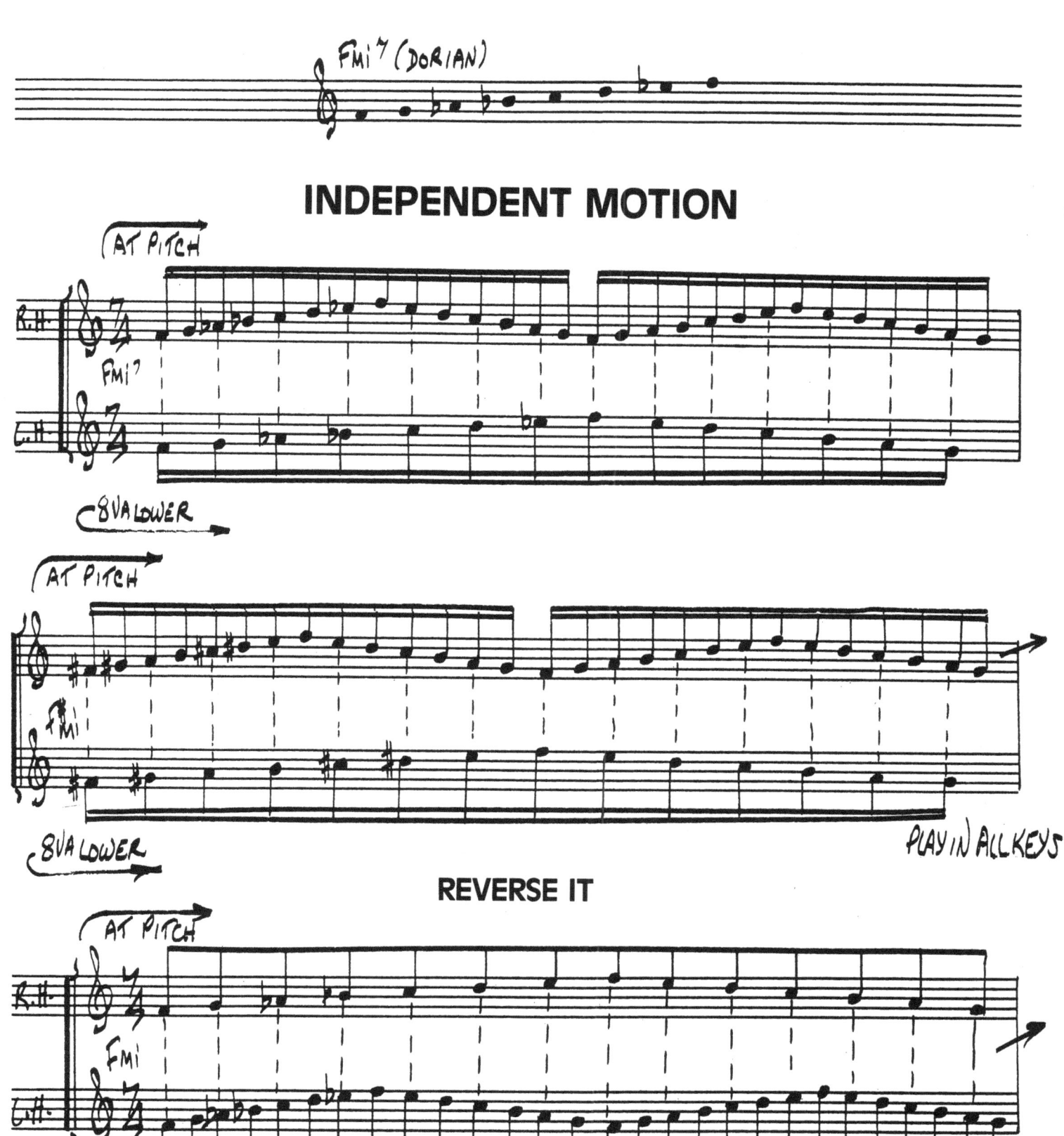

INDEPENDENT MOTION

REVERSE IT